salads

salads

MURDOCH BOOKS

Contents

Starters

Salata baladi

1½ tablespoons extra virgin olive oil
1½ tablespoons lemon juice
1 baby cos (romaine) lettuce,
   leaves torn
2 ripe tomatoes, each cut into
   8 wedges
1 small green capsicum (pepper),
   cut into bite-sized pieces
2 small Lebanese (short) cucumbers,
   seeded and chopped
4 radishes, sliced
1 small red onion, thinly sliced
2 tablespoons chopped flat-leaf
   (Italian) parsley
1 small handful mint leaves

In a bowl, whisk together the oil and lemon juice. Season well with salt and freshly cracked black pepper.

Put all the vegetables and herbs in a large serving bowl and toss well. Add the dressing and toss again. Serve at once, while the salad is crisp.

Serves 4

Borlotti bean, beetroot and mint salad

400 g (14 oz) tin borlotti beans,
    drained and rinsed (see Note)
450 g (1 lb) tin baby beetroot, drained
    and chopped
150 g (5 oz) cherry tomatoes, halved
1 handful mint leaves

Dressing
1 tablespoon apple cider vinegar or
    white wine vinegar
1 tablespoon olive oil

Put the beans, beetroot and cherry tomatoes in a serving dish. Roughly chop half the mint leaves and mix them through the salad. Whisk the dressing ingredients in a small bowl and season to taste. Pour over the salad and mix gently. Scatter over the remaining mint leaves and serve.

Note: When available, use fresh borlotti beans in this recipe. Blanch them in a pot of boiling water for several minutes until tender before combining with other ingredients.

Serves 4

Snow pea salad with Japanese dressing

200 g (7 oz) snow peas (mangetout), tailed
50 g (2 oz) snow pea (mangetout) sprouts
1 small red capsicum (pepper), julienned
2 teaspoon toasted sesame seeds

Japanese dressing
$1/2$ teaspoon dashi granules
1 tablespoon soy sauce
1 tablespoon mirin
1 teaspoon soft brown sugar
1 garlic clove, crushed
1 teaspoon finely chopped fresh ginger
$1/4$ teaspoon sesame oil
1 tablespoon vegetable oil
2 teaspoons toasted sesame seeds

Bring a pot of water to the boil, add snow peas and blanch for 1 minute. Drain and refresh under cold water, then drain again. Toss in a serving bowl with the snow pea sprouts and the capsicum.

To make dressing, dissolve dashi granules in $1 1/2$ tablespoons of hot water. Pour into a small bowl, add remaining dressing ingredients and whisk well. Pour the dressing over the snow peas, toss well and season to taste. Sprinkle with sesame seeds and serve.

Serves 4

Insalata caprese

3 large vine-ripened tomatoes, sliced
250 g (9 oz) bocconcini cheese,
   sliced (see Note)
16–20 whole basil leaves
3 tablespoons extra virgin olive oil

Arrange alternating slices of tomato and bocconcini on a serving platter. Slip the basil leaves in between the tomato and bocconcini slices. Drizzle with the oil, season well with salt and ground black pepper and serve.

Note: This popular salad is most successful when made with very fresh buffalo mozzarella, if you can find it. We've used bocconcini — small balls of fresh cow's milk mozzarella — in this recipe.

Serves 4

Moroccan eggplant with couscous

185 g (7 oz/1 cup) instant couscous
200 ml (7 fl oz) olive oil
1 onion, halved and sliced
1 eggplant (aubergine)
3 teaspoons ground cumin
1 1/2 teaspoons garlic salt
1/4 teaspoon ground cinnamon
1 teaspoon paprika
1/4 teaspoon ground cloves
50 g (2 oz) butter
2 1/2 large handfuls parsley, finely
    chopped
zest of 1 lemon
2 tablespoons capers, rinsed and
    drained

Put the couscous in a large bowl and add 375 ml (13 fl oz/1 1/2 cups) boiling water. Leave for 10 minutes, then fluff up with a fork.

Heat 2 tablespoons of oil in a large frying pan and gently cook the onion for 8–10 minutes, or until browned. Remove with a slotted spoon. Cut eggplant into 1 cm (1/2 inch) thick slices, then into quarters, and place in a large bowl. Mix cumin, garlic salt, cinnamon, paprika and cloves in a small bowl with 1/2 teaspoon of salt, then sprinkle over eggplant, tossing to coat well.

Heat the remaining oil in frying pan over medium heat. Add the eggplant and cook, turning once, for around 20–25 minutes, or until browned. Remove from the pan, allow to cool.

In the same pan, melt butter, then add the couscous and gently cook for 2–3 minutes. Stir in the onion, eggplant, parsley, lemon zest and capers. Cool to room temperature before serving.

Serves 4

Mezghaldi of onions with eggplant

4 onions
100 ml (3 fl oz) olive oil
1/2 teaspoon ground saffron threads
1 teaspoon ground ginger
1 teaspoon ground cinnamon
1/2 teaspoon ground allspice
1 1/2 tablespoons honey
600 g (1 lb 5 oz) long, thin eggplants
  (aubergines)

Halve the onions lengthways and cut into slender wedges. Put in a lidded frying pan, cover with cold water and bring to the boil. Cover and simmer for 5 minutes. Drain into a colander. Add 2 tablespoons of the olive oil to pan and, over low heat, stir in saffron, ginger, cinnamon and allspice. Cook for 1 minute, increase heat to medium and return onion to the pan.

Add the honey and 375 ml (13 fl oz/ 1 1/2 cups) water and season with salt and freshly ground black pepper. Stir well, reduce heat to low, cover and simmer for 40 minutes. Uncover and simmer for 10 minutes, or until most of the liquid has evaporated.

Wash and dry eggplants. Leaving the green stalks on, halve lengthways and peel off a strip of skin from underside of each half. Brush all halves on each side with the remaining oil. Cook in a heated chargrill pan or on a barbecue grill for 3–4 minutes each side until it is tender, adjusting the heat so it does not burn.

Arrange the eggplant cut side up on a platter or individual plates and season lightly with salt. Top with onion and pour over any juices from pan. Serve hot or warm with crusty bread.

Serves 4 as a side salad

Haloumi and asparagus salad with salsa verde

Salsa verde
1 small handful basil leaves
1 small handful mint leaves
1 large handful parsley leaves
1 tablespoon baby capers, rinsed
  and drained
1 garlic clove
1 tablespoon olive oil
2 teaspoons lemon juice
2 teaspoons lime juice

125 g (5 oz) haloumi cheese
175 g (6 oz) thin asparagus spears
1 tablespoon garlic oil or olive oil
50 g (2 oz) mixed salad leaves

To make the salsa verde, blend the herbs, capers, garlic and oil in a food processor until smooth. Add lemon and lime juice, and pulse briefly.

Heat a chargrill pan (griddle) to medium heat. Cut the haloumi into 1 cm (½ inch) slices, then cut each slice into two small triangles. Brush the haloumi and asparagus with the garlic oil. Chargrill the asparagus for 1 minute or until just tender, then the haloumi for 45 seconds on each side, or until grill marks appear.

Divide the salad leaves between two plates and top with the haloumi and the asparagus. Drizzle over the salsa verde just before serving.

Serves 2

Chicken noodle salad

100 g (4 oz) bean vermicelli noodles
1 tablespoon oil
1 garlic clove, crushed
3 cm (1 1/4 inch) piece of ginger,
  peeled and finely grated
1 green chilli, seeded and finely
  chopped
250 g (9 oz) minced (ground) chicken
  thighs
2 tablespoons lemon juice
2 makrut (kaffir lime) leaves, shredded
1 tablespoon fish sauce
1 tablespoon chilli sauce
2 tablespoons chopped coriander
  (cilantro) leaves

Put the noodles in a large heatproof bowl, cover with boiling water and soak for 5 minutes, or until softened. Alternatively, cook noodles according to the packet instructions. Drain the noodles well, then rinse under cold water and drain again.

Heat oil in a wok or frying pan over medium heat. Add garlic, ginger and chilli and stir-fry for about 1 minute, being careful not to burn garlic. Add the chicken and stir-fry for another 2–3 minutes. Stir in lemon juice, lime leaves, fish sauce and chilli sauce and stir-fry for a further minute. Remove from the heat and transfer to a bowl.

Cut noodles into shorter lengths with scissors. Add to the chicken mixture along with the coriander and mix well. Leave to cool completely, then divide between two plates.

Serves 2

Burghul, feta and parsley salad

90 g (3 oz/½ cup) burghul
  (bulgar) wheat
2 tablespoons chopped flat-leaf
  (Italian) parsley
2 tablespoons chopped mint
4 spring onions (scallions),
  finely chopped
2 firm ripe tomatoes, halved, seeded
  and diced
1 short (Lebanese) cucumber, halved,
  seeded and diced
100 g (4 oz) feta, crumbled
2 tablespoons lemon juice
2 tablespoons olive oil

Put burghul in a large bowl and add enough hot water to cover. Leave to soak for around 15–20 minutes, or until tender. Drain well, then squeeze out all the excess liquid.

Gently toss the burghul in a bowl with all the remaining ingredients. Season with sea salt and freshly ground black pepper and mix together well. Leave for at least one hour to allow flavours to mingle, then serve.

Serves 2

Tomato and bocconcini salad

Basil oil
125 ml (4 fl oz/½ cup) olive oil
1 large handful basil leaves, torn
1 tablespoon balsamic vinegar

3 Roma (plum) tomatoes, halved
175 g (6 oz) cherry bocconcini
  or baby mozzarella cheese
80 g (3 oz) mizuna lettuce leaves or
  baby rocket (arugula) leaves

To make basil oil, put the oil and basil leaves in a saucepan. Stir gently over medium heat for 3–5 minutes, or until very hot but not smoking. Remove from heat and discard basil. Reserve 1 tablespoon of the basil oil and mix it with vinegar; store remaining basil oil in a clean jar in the refrigerator to use in salad dressings and pasta sauces.

Arrange the tomato, bocconcini and lettuce on two plates. Drizzle with the basil oil and sprinkle with sea salt and cracked black pepper.

Serves 2

Vietnamese salad with lemongrass dressing

100 g (4 oz) dried rice vermicelli
1 small handful Vietnamese mint
  leaves, torn
1 small handful coriander
  (cilantro) leaves
1/2 small red onion, thinly sliced
1 small green mango, peeled
  and julienned
1/2 Lebanese (short) cucumber, halved
  and thinly sliced
80 g (3 oz/1/2 cup) crushed peanuts

Lemongrass dressing
3 tablespoons lime juice
2 teaspoons grated palm sugar or
  soft brown sugar
1 1/2 tablespoons seasoned rice
  vinegar
1 stem lemongrass, white part only,
  finely chopped
1 red chilli, seeded and finely
  chopped
1 makrut (kaffir lime) leaf, shredded

Put the noodles in a bowl, cover with boiling water and soak for 10 minutes, or until soft. Drain, rinse under cold water and then cut into short lengths. Toss in a large bowl with mint, onion, coriander, mango, the cucumber and three-quarters of the nuts. Divide the salad between plates.

Whisk the dressing ingredients and toss through the salad. Sprinkle the remaining nuts over the salad just before serving.

Serves 2

Buckwheat noodle salad with shiitake and snowpeas

125 g (5 oz) buckwheat noodles
2 tablespoons walnut pieces
1 tablespoon vegetable or olive oil
60 g (2 oz) fresh shiitake mushrooms,
  stalks discarded,
  caps thinly sliced
50 g (2 oz/½ cup) snow peas, tailed
  and finely sliced
3 spring onions (scallions),
  finely sliced

Sesame ginger dressing
1 tablespoon white wine vinegar
½ teaspoon sesame oil
2 tablespoons vegetable oil
2 cm (¾ inch) piece ginger, peeled
  and finely grated
1 small red chilli, seeded and
  finely chopped

Cook the noodles according to the packet instructions. Drain well, then rinse under running water, rubbing noodles together gently to remove some of the starch. Drain well, then place in a bowl.

Put a frying pan over high heat. Add walnuts and dry-fry for 2–3 minutes, shaking the pan now and then so the nuts colour evenly. Remove, leave to cool and roughly chop.

Heat the oil in the same pan, add the mushrooms and then sauté for about 2–3 minutes, or until tender. Add the mushrooms to the noodles with snow peas, spring onion and the chopped walnuts and gently mix together.

To make sesame ginger dressing, put vinegar, sesame oil and vegetable oil in a small bowl and whisk until well combined. Stir in the ginger and the chilli, then drizzle over noodles. Toss to combine, then divide the noodles between two plates. Serve them at room temperature.

Serves 2

Pasta salad with caramelised vegetables

2 tablespoons olive oil
2 celery stalks, sliced
1 small onion, halved and
  thinly sliced
1 garlic clove, crushed
pinch of sugar
2 leeks, white part only, sliced
175 g (6 oz) pasta shells or
  bows (see Note)
2 tablespoons toasted pine nuts
70 g (3 oz) soft blue cheese, such as
  gorgonzola, crumbled

Dressing
1 tablespoon olive oil
1 tablespoon chopped flat-leaf (Italian)
  parsley
1 tablespoon lemon juice

Heat oil in a frying pan. Add celery and onion, then cover and cook over medium heat for 5 minutes, stirring occasionally. Stir in garlic, sugar and leek. Reduce heat, cover the pan and gently cook, stirring occasionally, for a further 10 minutes, or until vegetables are golden brown and soft. Remove the lid, increase the heat and cook vegetables for another 2–3 minutes or until light golden, being careful not to burn them. Season to taste with salt and black pepper, then set aside.

Meanwhile, cook pasta in a large pot of rapidly boiling salted water until al dente. Drain well. While pasta is still warm, add caramelised vegetables and set aside.

Put dressing ingredients in a small bowl, season with salt and freshly ground black pepper and mix well. Pour over the pasta, stir in the pine nuts and cheese and toss gently. Leave to cool, then divide between two plates. This salad is delicious served cold, or warm.

Note: To save time, you could use 400 g (14 oz/about 2¼ cups) of cooked left-over pasta instead.

Serves 2

Rice salad with chicken

150 g (5 oz/¾ cup) jasmine rice (see
 Note)
100 g (4 oz) roast or barbecued
 chicken
½ Lebanese (short) cucumber,
 seeded and diced
250 g (9 oz) grape tomatoes, halved
4 spring onions (scallions), sliced
310 g (11 oz) tin corn kernels, drained

Dressing
3 tablespoons olive oil
1 tablespoon lemon juice
1 tablespoon runny honey
1 teaspoon Dijon mustard
1 small red chilli, seeded and sliced

Cook rice in a pot of boiling water
until just tender. Drain well, rinse
under cold water, then drain again.
Leave in a sieve over a saucepan,
fluffing up the grains every now and
again with a fork. While rice is still
warm, place it in a bowl while you
make the dressing.

Combine all the dressing ingredients
together thoroughly in a small bowl,
season with salt and black pepper
and pour over warm rice. Mix well,
cover and refrigerate until cooled
completely.

Shred the chicken into bite-sized
pieces and mix through the rice with
the cucumber, tomato, spring onion
and corn kernels. Check seasoning,
then divide between two plates.

Serves 2

Note: You could use 440 g (1 lb/
2⅓ cups) of cold cooked rice instead.

Grilled tofu with broccoli and sesame dressing

200 g (7 oz) broccoli, cut
    into florets
100 g (4 oz) baby corn, halved
    lengthways
80 g (3 oz) snow peas (mangetout),
    tailed
1 large red capsicum (pepper), sliced
200 g (7 oz) smoked tofu, cut into
    5 mm (^{1}/4 inch) thick slices

Sesame dressing
3 tablespoons olive oil
2 teaspoons sesame oil
2 tablespoons lemon juice

Bring a pot of water to the boil and add a teaspoon of salt. Add broccoli and cook for 30 seconds, then add the corn and snow peas and cook for 1 more minute. Drain, refresh under cold water, then plunge into a bowl of cold water to cool. Drain well and toss in a serving dish with capsicum.

Whisk dressing ingredients together in a small bowl. Pour half the dressing over the salad and then gently toss to combine well.

Heat a barbecue grill or chargrill pan (griddle) to medium. Add the tofu and cook for 2 minutes on each side, or until grill marks appear. Add to salad with remaining dressing, toss gently and serve.

Serves 4

Spinach and sweet potato salad with orange-sesame dressing

1 pitta bread
3 tablespoons olive oil
500 g (1 lb 2 oz) orange sweet potato
    unpeeled, cut into slices
    1 cm (½ inch) thick
1 small orange
150 g (5 oz) baby spinach

Dressing
3 tablespoons olive oil
1 teaspoon sesame oi
2 tablespoons orange juice
1 teaspoon lemon juice
1 teaspoon orange zest, finely grated
1 clove garlic, crushed
2 teaspoons Dijon mustard

Preheat a grill (broiler) to high. Cut off and discard the edge of the bread. Split the bread into 2 thin halves, and lightly brush all over with some of the oil. Toast under the grill until crisp and lightly browned. Reserve.

Toss sweet potato in the remaining oil and grill until soft and golden on both sides, 8–10 minutes. Transfer to a salad bowl.

Peel orange, removing all the pith. To fillet segments, hold orange over a bowl and use a knife to cut down either side of membranes. Put the segments in the bowl and add the spinach. Break up pitta crisps into small shards and put into the bowl. Toss lightly.

Put all the dressing ingredients in a small bowl and whisk to combine. Season with salt and freshly ground black pepper, to taste. Pour over the salad just before serving.

Serves 4

Radicchio with figs and ginger vinaigrette

1 radicchio lettuce
1 baby frisée (curly endive)
3 oranges (see Note)
1/2 small red onion, thinly
   sliced into rings
8 small green figs, quartered
3 tablespoons extra virgin olive oil
1 teaspoon red wine vinegar
1/8 teaspoon ground cinnamon
2 tablespoons orange juice
2 tablespoons very finely chopped
   glacé ginger, with 2 teaspoon syrup
2 pomegranates (optional), sliced in
   half

Wash the radicchio and frisée leaves thoroughly and drain well. Tear any large leaves into bite-sized pieces and toss in a salad bowl. Peel and then segment the oranges, discarding all the bitter white pith. Add to the salad leaves with onion and figs, reserving eight fig quarters.

Whisk oil, vinegar, cinnamon, orange juice, ginger and the ginger syrup in a small jug. Season to taste, pour over the salad and toss lightly.

Arrange reserved figs in pairs over the salad. If you are using pomegranates, scoop out the seeds, scatter over the top and serve.

Serves 4

Note: When in season use mandarins and mandarin juice instead of oranges and orange juice.

Soba noodle salad with tahini dressing

300 g (11 oz) snake beans or green beans
300 g (11 oz) soba noodles
4 spring onions (scallions), finely sliced
1 tablespoon black sesame seeds

Tahini dressing
1 ½ tablespoons tahini
2 small garlic cloves, crushed
3 tablespoons rice vinegar
3 tablespoons olive oil
1 teaspoon sesame oil
2 teaspoons soy sauce
1 tablespoon sugar

Trim beans and cut into long strips on the diagonal. Bring a pot of lightly salted water to the boil, add beans and blanch until just tender, for about 2–3 minutes. Drain, refresh the beans under cold water, then drain again. Cook noodles in a large pot of boiling water for 3–4 minutes, or until tender. Drain, refresh under cold water, then drain again.

Put all the tahini dressing ingredients in a screw-top jar with 1 tablespoon of warm water and shake vigorously to combine. Season to taste.

Combine the beans, noodles, spring onion and sesame seeds in a large serving bowl. When you're ready to eat, add the dressing and lightly toss together. Serve at once.

Serves 4

Pumpkin and prawn salad with rocket

800 g (1 lb 12 oz) pumpkin, peeled
and cut into 3 cm (1¼ inch) cubes
2 small red onions, cut into
thick wedges
1 tablespoon oil
2 cloves garlic, crushed
500 g (11 oz) cooked
prawns (shrimp), peeled
and deveined
200 g (7 oz) baby rocket (arugula)
leaves
1–2 tablespoons balsamic vinegar
1 tablespoon olive oil

Preheat oven to 200°C (400°F/Gas 6).
Toss the pumpkin and onion in a large
bowl with the oil and garlic. Spread in
a single layer on a baking tray and
then bake for 25–30 minutes, or until
tender. Transfer to a serving bowl,
add the prawns and rocket and gently
toss together.

Whisk the vinegar and the oil together
and season to taste with sea salt and
freshly ground black pepper. Drizzle
over the salad and serve.

Serves 4

Chicken and spring vegetable salad

600 g (1 lb 5 oz) chicken breast fillets
½ lime, juiced
4 kaffir (makrut) lime leaves, shredded
½ onion, peeled
6 black peppercorns
175 g (6 oz) asparagus
175 g (6 oz) broad (fava) beans,
    defrosted if frozen
225 g (8 oz) baby green beans

Lemon tarragon dressing
1 tablespoon olive oil
2 tablespoons lemon juice
2 tablespoons chopped tarragon
    leaves

Half-fill a large pot with water. Add the chicken, lime juice, lime leaves, onion and peppercorns. Cover and bring to the boil, then reduce heat and simmer for 3 minutes. Turn off heat and leave chicken to cool in broth for at least 30 minutes — it will continue to cook.

Combine the dressing ingredients in a small bowl. Season lightly with salt and pepper, mix well and set aside. Snap woody ends off asparagus and discard. Bring another pot of water to the boil and add a pinch of salt. Add broad beans and cook for 1 minute, then add green beans and simmer for 1 minute. Now add the asparagus and cook for a further minute. Drain well and refresh under cold water. Drain well again.

Slice asparagus spears lengthways and place them in a serving dish with green beans. Remove skins from the broad beans and add them to serving dish. Remove cooled chicken from poaching liquid. Shred the fillets, then gently toss them through salad with the dressing. Serve at once.

Serves 4

Roasted tomato and pasta salad with pesto

140 ml (5 fl oz) olive oil
500 g (1 lb 2 oz) cherry tomatoes
5 garlic cloves, unpeeled
400 g (14 oz) orecchiette or other
  shell-shaped pasta
90 g (3 oz/⅓ cup) ready-made pesto
3 tablespoons balsamic vinegar
basil leaves, to serve

Preheat oven to 180°C (350°F/Gas 4). Put 2 tablespoons of oil in a roasting tin and leave to warm in the hot oven for 5 minutes. Add cherry tomatoes and garlic, season well and toss until the tomatoes are well coated. Return to the oven and roast for 20 minutes (be sure to keep all the pan juices for the dressing).

Meanwhile, cook the pasta in a large pot of rapidly boiling salted water until al dente. Drain well and transfer to a large serving bowl.

Squeeze flesh from the roasted garlic cloves into a bowl. Add the remaining oil, pesto, vinegar and 3 tablespoons of the pan juices from the roasted tomatoes. Season with a little salt and pepper, then toss to combine. Add to the pasta and mix well to coat. Gently stir in roasted tomatoes, then scatter with basil leaves. Serve warm or cold.

Serves 4

Mushroom and shredded chicken salad

1–2 tablespoons olive oil
200 g (7 oz) small button mushrooms
200 g (7 oz) other mixed mushrooms
  (such as Swiss brown and shiitake),
  larger ones halved or quartered
400 g (14 oz) cooked chicken,
  shredded
200 g (7 oz) mixed salad leaves

Lime and soy dressing
2 tablespoons lime juice
1 tablespoon soy sauce
2 tablespoons olive oil
1 tablespoon sweet chilli sauce
1 tablespoon red wine vinegar

Heat 1 tablespoon of the oil in a frying pan. Add mushrooms and cook over medium heat for 2–3 minutes, or until softened. Toss in a large bowl with the shredded chicken.

Combine all the lime and soy dressing ingredients in a small bowl or jug, mix well and then pour two-thirds over the warm mushrooms.

Arrange the salad leaves in a serving dish and toss through the remaining dressing. Top with the chicken and mushrooms and serve warm.

Serves 4

Couscous and chargrilled vegetable salad

1 small eggplant (aubergine), sliced
1 red capsicum (pepper), sliced
1 green capsicum (pepper), sliced
2 zucchini (courgettes), sliced
1 red onion, sliced
2 tablespoons extra virgin olive oil
1 tablespoon sesame oil
115 g (4 oz) instant couscous
500 ml (17 fl oz/2 cups) hot vegetable
  stock
3 cloves garlic, crushed
3 tablespoons low-salt soy sauce
3 tablespoons lemon juice
3 tablespoons finely shredded
  fresh mint
crusty bread, to serve

Put eggplant, capsicum, zucchini and onion into a bowl, drizzle with the oil and toss to combine. Cook over a chargrill (broiler) until the vegetables are tender.

Put the couscous into a bowl, pour over the hot stock and allow to stand for 10 minutes or until all the liquid is absorbed. Use a fork to separate the grains. Add the vegetables, combined soy, lemon juice and mint and gently toss to combine. Serve the warm salad with crusty bread.

Serves 4

Prawn and fennel salad

1.25 kg (2 lb 12 oz) raw large prawns
  (shrimp), peeled and deveined
1 large fennel bulb (400 g/14 oz),
  thinly sliced
300 g (11 oz) watercress
2 tablespoons finely chopped chives
125 ml (4 fl oz/½ cup) extra virgin
  olive oil
3 tablespoons lemon juice
1 tablespoon Dijon mustard
1 large garlic clove, finely chopped

Bring a saucepan of water to the boil,
then add prawns, return to the boil
and simmer for 2 minutes, or until the
prawns turn pink and are cooked
through. Drain and leave to cool. Pat
the prawns dry with paper towels and
slice in half lengthways. Place them in
a large serving bowl. Add watercress,
the fennel and the chives to the bowl
and mix well.

To make the dressing, whisk the oil,
the lemon juice, mustard and garlic
together. Pour the dressing over the
salad, season with salt and cracked
black pepper and toss gently. Arrange
the salad on serving plates and serve.

Serves 4

Roast mushroom and baby bean salad

600 g (1 lb 5 oz) field mushrooms, brushed clean
2 tablespoons olive oil
3 cloves garlic, crushed
2 tablespoons lemon juice
6 French shallots, root ends trimmed, skin left on
1½ tablespoons tarragon vinegar
2 teaspoons finely chopped tarragon
1 tablespoon finely chopped flat-leaf (Italian) parsley
200 g (7 oz) baby green beans, trimmed
2 handfuls rocket (arugula)

Preheat oven to 200°C (400°F/Gas 6). Place the mushrooms in a single layer in a large roasting pan. Add oil, garlic, lemon juice and shallots and toss until coated. Roast for around 30 minutes, occasionally spooning over the juices.

Remove from the oven and cool to room temperature. Slip shallots from their skins and discard skin. Pour the cooking juices into a large mixing bowl. Add tarragon vinegar, tarragon and parsley. Mix and season well.

Blanch beans in boiling salted water for 2 minutes, or until just tender. Drain well and, while still hot, add to the dressing. Allow to cool to room temperature.

Cut the mushrooms into quarters, or eighths if large, and add to the beans with the shallots and rocket. Gently toss together and serve.

Serves 4

Pear and bean salad

2 pears, unpeeled, cored and
    chopped
45 g (1¹/₂ oz/¹/₂ cup) bean sprouts
125 g (5 oz/1 cup) sliced, cooked
    green beans
4 spring onions (scallions), chopped
125 g (5 oz) tin red kidney beans,
    drained and rinsed
100 g (4 oz/¹/₂ cup) drained
    and rinsed tinned soya beans,
    or use frozen
1 tablespoon poppy seeds

Dressing
3 tablespoons olive oil
1 teaspoon white vinegar
¹/₂ teaspoon sugar
1 garlic clove, crushed

Combine the pears, bean sprouts,
green beans, spring onions, kidney
beans and soya beans in a large bowl.
Combine gently.

To make dressing, combine oil, sugar,
vinegar, sugar and 3 tablespoons of
water. Taste for seasoning, then pour
over the vegetables. Chill the salad for
1 hour before serving. Sprinkle with
poppy seeds just before serving.

Note: This salad is best made the day
before serving and stored overnight in
the refrigerator to enable the flavours
to develop more fully.

Serves 4

Fresh beetroot and goat's cheese salad

1 kg (2 lb 4 oz) fresh beetroot (about
   4 bulbs with leaves)
200 g (7 oz) green beans
1 tablespoon red wine vinegar
2 tablespoons extra virgin olive oil
1 clove garlic, crushed
1 tablespoon drained capers,
   coarsely chopped
100 g (4 oz) goat's cheese

Trim leaves from the beetroot. Scrub the bulbs and wash the leaves well. Simmer bulbs in a large saucepan of boiling water, covered, for 30 minutes, or until tender when pierced with the point of a knife. (Cooking time may vary depending on size of the bulbs.)

Meanwhile, bring a saucepan of water to the boil, add the beans and cook for 3 minutes, or until tender. Remove with a slotted spoon and plunge into a bowl of cold water. Drain well. Add beetroot leaves to the same saucepan of boiling water and then cook for 3–5 minutes, or until the leaves and stems are tender. Drain, plunge into a bowl of water, then drain again well.

Cool the beetroots, then, wearing gloves, peel off the skins and cut the bulbs into thin wedges.

Divide the beans and beetroot (leaves and bulbs) among four serving plates. Crumble goat's cheese over the top and drizzle with dressing.

Serves 4

Caramelised onion and potato salad

oil, for cooking
6 red onions, thinly sliced
1 kg (2 lb 4 oz) small waxy potatoes,
    unpeeled
4 slices bacon, rind removed
30 g (1 oz/²⁄₃ cup) snipped chives
250 g (9 oz/1 cup) mayonnaise
1 tablespoon Dijon mustard
juice of 1 lemon
2 tablespoons sour cream

Heat 2 tablespoons of oil in a large heavy-based frying pan, add onion and cook over medium-low heat for 40 minutes, or until very soft.Cut the potatoes into large chunks (if small, leave whole). Cook in boiling water for 10 minutes, or until just tender, then drain and cool them slightly. (Do not overcook or they will fall apart.)

Grill (broil) bacon until crisp, drain on paper towels and cool slightly before coarsely chopping. Put potato, onion and chives in a large bowl, reserving a few chives for a garnish, and mix well.

Put mayonnaise, mustard, lemon juice and sour cream in a bowl and whisk together. Pour over the salad and toss to coat. Sprinkle with the bacon and garnish with chives.

Serves 10

Potato and prawn salad

800 g (1 lb 12 oz) waxy potatoes
  (such as chats, pink fir apple
  or kipfler), scrubbed
650 g (1 lb 7 oz) large raw prawns
  (shrimp), peeled and deveined,
  tails intact
200 g (7 oz/2 small bunches) rocket
  (arugula), leaves trimmed and torn
2 avocados, diced

Red wine vinegar dressing
125 ml (4 fl oz/$\frac{1}{2}$ cup) olive oil
3 tablespoons red wine vinegar
2 teaspoons mustard powder
2 tablespoons finely chopped dill

Put potatoes in a large pot of salted
water and bring to the boil. Reduce
the heat and simmer rapidly for
12–15 minutes, or until tender when
pierced with a sharp knife. Drain well,
cool a little, then slice large potatoes,
keeping small ones whole. Transfer to
a serving dish.

Whisk dressing ingredients together
in a small bowl until well combined.
Season with salt and black pepper
and pour two-thirds of dressing over
potatoes. Toss gently and set aside.

Meanwhile, preheat a barbecue grill
or chargrill pan (griddle) to high. Cook
prawns for 2 minutes on one side, or
until just starting to turn pink. Turn
and cook for 1 minute more, or until
just cooked through. Add to potatoes,
with rocket and avocado. Pour over
the remaining dressing, toss gently
and serve at once.

Note: This salad can also be served
cold. If you're making it in advance,
dress potatoes with two-thirds of the
dressing, but mix through avocado,
rocket and remaining dressing just
before serving.

Serves 4

Cucumber and radish salsa with crisp-skinned salmon

Salsa
1 large cucumber
2 stalks celery, thinly sliced
1 French shallot, diced
1 avocado, diced
20 baby white and/or red radishes,
  halved, or quartered if large
1 small handful coriander (cilantro)

Dressing
80 ml (3 fl oz/⅓ cup) olive oil
2 tablespoons lime juice
1 teaspoon finely grated lime zest
1 clove garlic, crushed
1 teaspoon honey

4 small fillets salmon, skin on
2–3 tablespoons olive oil
1 small handful coriander (cilantro)

To make the salsa, peel the cucumber and cut in half lengthways. Scoop out and discard seeds, using a teaspoon. Slice thinly into half-moon shapes, put in a large bowl. Add celery, shallot, avocado, radishes and coriander.

To make the dressing, put the oil, lime juice, lime zest, garlic and honey in a small bowl and mix well. Season with salt and freshly ground black pepper.

Brush the salmon lightly with olive oil and sprinkle the skin with a little salt. Heat the remaining oil in a large frying pan over high heat. When hot, add the salmon, skin side down, and hold a spatula or another frying pan on top of the fillets to keep them flat. Fry for 1–2 minutes, or until the skin is crisp and brown all over. Reduce the heat to medium and turn salmon. Cook for 2–3 minutes, depending on the thickness, or until just until opaque, Drain on paper towels.

When cool enough to handle, use the scissors to cut each salmon fillet across the grain into 3 strips. Break each strip into bite-sized pieces of several flakes. Add to salsa, along with dressing and coriander. Toss gently to coat, and serve.

Serves 4

Asparagus and mushroom salad

155 g (5 oz) asparagus spears
1 tablespoon wholegrain mustard
3 tablespoons orange juice
2 tablespoons lemon juice
1 tablespoon lime juice
1 tablespoon orange zest
2 teaspoons lemon zest
2 teaspoons lime zest
2 cloves garlic, crushed
90 g (3 oz/¼ cup) honey
400 g (14 oz) button mushrooms, halved
150 g (5 oz) rocket
1 red capsicum (pepper), cut into strips

Snap woody ends from the asparagus spears and cut in half on the diagonal. Cook in boiling water for 1 minute, or until just tender. Drain, plunge into cold water and set aside. Place the mustard, citrus juice and zest, garlic and honey in a large saucepan and season with pepper. Bring to the boil, reduce heat and add the mushrooms, tossing for 2 minutes. Cool.

Remove the mushrooms from sauce with a slotted spoon. Return sauce to the heat, bring to the boil, reduce the heat and simmer for 3–5 minutes, or until reduced and syrupy. Cool slightly.

Toss the mushrooms, rocket leaves, capsicum and asparagus. Put on a plate and drizzle with the sauce.

Serves 4

Spinach, apricot and avocado salad with mixed seed dressing

150 g (5 oz) baby spinach leaves
175 g (6 oz) trimmed watercress
100 g (4 oz) dried apricots,
  roughly chopped
100 g (4 oz) parmesan, shaved
2 avocados, cut into thick slices
100 g (4 oz) mung bean sprouts
3 tablespoons sunflower seeds
2 tablespoons sesame seeds
1 tablespoon extra virgin olive oil
2 tablespoons orange juice
2 tablespoons balsamic vinegar
1 teaspoon honey
2 cloves garlic, crushed
French stick, to serve

Arrange the spinach, the watercress, apricots, parmesan and avocado on a large salad platter. Combine sprouts and seeds and sprinkle them over the salad. Whisk together the oil, orange juice, balsamic vinegar, honey and the garlic and drizzle over salad, gently tossing to combine. Serve at once with a piece of French stick.

Serves 6

Stuffed mushroom salad

20 button mushrooms
1/4 cup (60 g/2 oz) pesto, chilled
100 g (3½ oz) rocket leaves
1 green oakleaf lettuce
12 small black olives
1/3 cup (50 g/1 3/4 oz) sliced semi-dried
   or sun-dried tomatoes
1 tablespoon roughly chopped basil
parmesan shavings, to serve

Dressing
1/3 cup (80 ml/2 3/4 fl oz) olive oil
1 tablespoon white wine vinegar
1 teaspoon Dijon mustard

Trim mushroom stalks level with the caps and scoop out the remaining stalk with a melon baller. Spoon the pesto into the mushrooms.

To make the dressing, whisk together all the ingredients. Season with salt and pepper, to taste.

Arrange the rocket and lettuce leaves on a serving plate and top with the mushrooms, olives, tomato and basil. Drizzle dressing over the salad and top with parmesan shavings. Serve immediately.

Serves 4

Spicy lentil salad

220 g (7 oz/1 cup) brown rice
185 g (6 oz/1 cup) brown lentils
1 teaspoon turmeric
1 teaspoon ground cinnamon
6 cardamom pods
3 star anise
2 bay leaves
3 tablespoons sunflower oil
1 tablespoon lemon juice
250 g (9 oz) broccoli florets
2 carrots, cut into julienne strips
1 onion, finely chopped
2 cloves garlic, crushed
1 red capsicum (pepper), finely
   chopped
1 teaspoon garam masala
1 teaspoon ground coriander
250 g (9 oz/1½ cups) fresh or frozen
   peas, thawed

Mint and yoghurt dressing
250 g (8 oz/1 cup) plain yoghurt
1 tablespoon lemon juice
1 tablespoon chopped fresh mint
1 teaspoon cumin seeds

Put 750 ml (24 fl oz/3 cups) water with rice, lentils, turmeric, cinnamon, cardamom, star anise and bay leaves in a pan. Stir well and bring to the boil. Reduce heat, cover and simmer gently for 50–60 minutes, or until the liquid is absorbed. Remove the whole spices. Transfer the mixture to a large bowl. Whisk 2 tablespoons of the oil with the lemon juice and fork through the rice mixture.

Boil, steam or microwave the broccoli and carrots until tender. Drain and refresh in cold water.

Heat remaining oil in a large pan and add the onion, garlic and capsicum. Stir-fry for 2–3 minutes, then add the garam masala and coriander, and stir-fry for a further 1–2 minutes. Add the vegetables and toss to coat in spice mixture. Add to rice and fork through to combine.

Cover and refrigerate until cold. To make the dressing, mix the yoghurt, lemon juice, mint and cumin seeds together, and season with salt and pepper. Spoon salad into individual serving bowls or onto a platter and serve with the dressing.

Serves 6

Squid salad with salsa verde

800 g (1 lb 12 oz) smallish squid,
 cleaned, scored and sliced into
 4 cm (1½ inch) diamonds
2 tablespoons olive oil
2 tablespoons lime juice
150 g (5 oz) green beans, trimmed
 and halved
175 g (6 oz) snow peas (mangetout),
 tailed
100 g (4 oz) baby rocket (arugula)
 leaves

Salsa verde
1 thick slice white bread, crusts
 removed
140 ml (5 fl oz) olive oil
3 tablespoons finely chopped parsley
2 teaspoons finely grated lemon zest
3 tablespoons lemon juice
2 anchovy fillets, finely chopped
2 tablespoons capers, rinsed and
 drained
1 garlic clove, crushed

Toss the squid in a bowl with the oil, lime juice and a little salt and pepper. Cover with plastic wrap, refrigerate and leave to marinate for 2 hours. To make the salsa verde, break the bread into chunks and drizzle with 2 tablespoons of the oil, mixing it in with your hands so it is absorbed.

Place bread and remaining oil in a food processor with remaining salsa verde ingredients, and blend to a paste. If mixture is too thick, thin it with a extra lemon juice and olive oil.

Bring a pot of lightly salted water to the boil, add beans and blanch until tender, about 2–3 minutes. Remove with tongs, refresh under cold water, then drain well. Blanch snow peas in the same pot for 1 minute, then drain, refresh in cold water and drain again.

Meanwhile, preheat a barbecue grill or chargrill pan (griddle) to high. Cook the squid in batches for 3 minutes per batch, or until cooked. Take off the heat, allow to cool slightly and toss in a bowl with the beans, the snow peas and rocket. Add 3 tablespoons of salsa verde and toss gently. Arrange on a serving platter, drizzle with the remaining salsa verde and serve.

Serves 4

Chicken with green chilli salsa verde

Green chilli salsa verde
1 green capsicum (pepper), roughly chopped
1–2 long green chillies, seeded and chopped
1 garlic clove, chopped
1 handful flat-leaf (Italian) parsley
1 handful basil
3 spring onions (scallions), finely chopped
1 tablespoon lemon juice
1 tablespoon olive oil

4 chicken breast fillets (about 200 g/7 oz each)
70 g (3 oz/2⅓ cups) watercress sprigs
3 celery stalks, sliced

To make salsa verde, put capsicum, chilli, garlic, parsley and the basil in a food processor and blend to a purée. Transfer mixture to a sieve and leave to sit for 20 minutes to drain, then transfer to a bowl and stir in spring onion, the lemon juice and oil. Season with salt and black pepper. Preheat a barbecue grill or chargrill pan (griddle) to medium.

Add chicken to the pan and cook for 6–8 minutes on one side. Turn and cook for a further 5 minutes, or until cooked through — the exact cooking time will vary depending on the heat of your barbecue and the thickness of your chicken fillets. Leave to cool slightly, then shred into a large bowl.

While the chicken is still warm, add the salsa verde and toss to coat well. Combine the watercress and celery in a serving dish, top with the chicken and salsa verde mixture, toss gently and serve at once.

Serves 4

Artichoke, prosciutto and rocket salad

4 artichokes
2 eggs, lightly beaten
20 g (1 oz/¼ cup) fresh breadcrumbs
25 g (1 oz/¼ cup) grated parmesan
  cheese
olive oil for frying, plus 1 tablespoon
  extra
8 slices prosciutto
3 teaspoons white wine vinegar
1 garlic clove, crushed
150 g (5 oz) rocket (arugula), long
  stalks trimmed
shaved parmesan cheese, optional
sea salt

Bring a large saucepan of water to the boil. Remove the outer leaves of each artichoke, trim stem and cut 2–3 cm (¾–1¼ inches) off the top. Cut into quarters and remove the 'choke'. Boil pieces for 2 minutes, then drain.

Whisk eggs in a bowl and combine the seasoned breadcrumbs and the parmesan in another bowl. Dip each artichoke quarter into egg, then roll in the crumb mixture to coat. Fill a frying pan with olive oil to a depth of 2 cm (¾ inch) and heat over medium heat.

Add artichokes in batches and fry for 2–3 minutes, or until golden. Remove from pan and drain on paper towels. Heat 1 tablespoon of olive oil in a non-stick frying pan over medium–high heat. Cook prosciutto in two batches for 2 minutes, or until it is crisp and golden. Remove from pan, reserving the oil.

Combine reserved oil, vinegar and the garlic with a little salt and pepper. Place rocket in a bowl, add half of the salad dressing and toss well. Divide the rocket, artichokes and prosciutto among four plates, and drizzle with the remaining dressing. Garnish with shaved parmesan, if desired, and sprinkle with sea salt.

Serves 4

Fusilli salad with sherry vinaigrette

300 g (11 oz) fusilli
250 g (9 oz/2 cups) cauliflower florets
125 ml (4 fl oz/½ cup) olive oil
16 slices pancetta
10 g (½ oz/½ cup) small sage leaves
100 g (4 oz/⅔ cup) pine nuts, toasted
2 tablespoons finely chopped red
  Asian shallots
1½ tablespoons sherry vinegar
1 small red chilli, finely chopped
2 garlic cloves, crushed
1 teaspoon soft brown sugar
2 tablespoons orange juice
15 g (½ oz/¾ cup) parsley, finely
  chopped
35 g (½ oz/⅓ cup) shaved parmesan
  cheese

Cook the fusilli in a large saucepan of boiling, salted water for 12 minutes, or until al dente. Drain and refresh under cold water until it is cool. Drain well. Blanch the cauliflower florets in boiling water for 3 minutes, then drain and cool.

Heat 1 tablespoon of oil in a non-stick frying pan and cook the pancetta for 2 minutes, or until crisp. Drain on paper towels. Add 1 more tablespoon of the oil and cook the sage leaves for 1 minute, or until they are crisp. Drain on paper towels. In a large serving bowl, combine the pasta, pine nuts, and the cauliflower.

Heat remaining olive oil, add shallots and cook gently for 2 minutes, or until soft. Remove from the heat then add the vinegar, chilli, garlic, brown sugar, orange juice and the chopped parsley. Pour warm dressing over pasta and toss gently to combine.

Place the salad in a serving bowl. Crumble the pancetta over the top and scatter with sage leaves and shaved parmesan. Serve warm.

Serves 6

Seafood salad

500 g (1 lb 2 oz) small squid
1 kg (2 lb 4 oz) large clams
1 kg (2 lb 4 oz) black mussels
500 g (1 lb 2 oz) raw medium prawns
    (shrimp), peeled, deveined,
    tails intact
1 very large chopped flat-leaf (Italian)
    parsley

Dressing
2 tablespoons lemon juice
80 ml (3 fl oz/$\frac{1}{3}$ cup) olive oil
1 garlic clove, crushed

Gently pull apart body and tentacles of the squid to separate. Remove the head by cutting below the eyes. Push out the beak and discard. Pull quill from the body of squid and discard. Under cold running water, pull away all skin (the flaps can be used). Rinse well, then slice the squid into rings.

Scrub clams and mussels and remove beards. Discard any that are cracked or don't close when tapped. Rinse under running water. Fill a saucepan with 2 cm ($\frac{3}{4}$ inches) water, add the clams and mussels, cover, and boil for 4–5 minutes, or until shells open. Remove, reserving liquid. Discard any that do not open. Remove from shells and place in a bowl.

Bring 1 litre (35 fl oz/4 cups) water to the boil and add prawns and squid. Cook for 3–4 minutes, or until prawns turn pink and squid is tender. Drain and add to the clams and mussels.

To make the dressing, whisk all the ingredients together. Season. Pour over seafood, add parsley, reserving 1 tablespoon and toss to coat. Cover and refrigerate for 30–40 minutes. Sprinkle with remaining parsley and serve with fresh bread.

Serves 4

Prawn and cannellini bean salad

200 g (7 oz/1 cup) dried
  cannellini beans
2 red capsicums (peppers)
300 g (11 oz) baby green beans
½ loaf day-old ciabatta or other
  crusty bread
80 ml (3 fl oz/⅓ cup) olive oil
1 large garlic clove, finely chopped
1 kg (2 lb 4 oz) raw prawns (shrimp),
  peeled and deveined, tails intact
1 large handful flat-leaf (Italian)
  parsley, roughly chopped

Lemon and caper dressing
3 tablespoons lemon juice
3 tablespoons olive oil
2 tablespoons capers, rinsed, drained
  and chopped
1 teaspoon sugar, optional

Soak cannellini beans in cold water for 8 hours, or overnight. Drain beans, then put them in a pot and cover with water. Bring to the boil, reduce the heat and simmer for 20–30 minutes, or until tender. Drain and rinse.

Cut capsicums into large flat pieces and remove seeds and membranes. Cook, skin-side-up, under a hot grill (broiler) until skins blacken and blister. Leave to cool in a plastic bag, then peel skin and cut the flesh into strips. Add to the cannellini beans. Bring a saucepan of lightly salted water to the boil, add green beans and blanch until bright green and just tender. Drain and add to serving bowl.

Put all the dressing ingredients in a screw-top jar and shake well. Season to taste and set aside. Cut the bread into six slices, then cut each slice into quarters. Heat 3 tablespoons of oil in a frying pan and fry bread slices over medium heat for a minute or two on each side until golden. Remove.

Heat remaining oil in frying pan, add garlic and prawns and then cook for 2–3 minutes. Toss prawns through the salad with dressing, toasted bread and parsley and serve.

Serves 4

Herbed feta salad

2 slices thick white bread
200 g (7 oz) feta cheese
1 clove garlic, crushed
1 tablespoon chopped marjoram
1 tablespoon snipped chives
1 tablespoon chopped fresh basil
2 tablespoons white wine vinegar
80 ml (3 fl oz/⅓ cup) olive oil
1 red coral lettuce
1 green mignonette or oakleaf lettuce

Preheat the oven to 180°C (350°F/ Gas 4). Remove the crusts from the bread and cut the bread into small cubes. Place on an oven tray in a single layer and bake for 10 minutes, until crisp and lightly golden. Transfer to a bowl and cool completely.

Cut feta into small cubes and put in a bowl. Put garlic, marjoram, chives, basil, vinegar and oil in a screw-top jar and shake well. Pour over feta and cover with plastic wrap. Leave for at least 30 minutes, stirring occasionally.

Tear lettuce into large pieces and put in a serving bowl. Add feta with the dressing and bread cubes and toss the salad well.

Serves 8

Roast cherry tomato and chicken salad

250 g (9 oz) cherry tomatoes or small
  truss tomatoes
2 garlic cloves, unpeeled
1 tablespoon olive oil
1 thyme sprig, cut into 3 pieces
1 barbecued chicken
100 g (4 oz) baby rocket (arugula)
  leaves
2 tablespoons capers, rinsed and
  drained, optional
1 tablespoon balsamic vinegar

Preheat oven to 180°C (350°F/Gas 4).
Put tomatoes, whole garlic cloves, oil
and thyme in a roasting tin and bake
for 15 minutes. Meanwhile, remove
meat from the chicken, discarding the
skin and bones. Shred meat and toss
in a bowl with the rocket and capers.

Allow the cooked tomatoes to cool
slightly, then gently squash each one
to release some of the juice. Add the
tomatoes to chicken mixture, leaving
the garlic and pan juices in roasting
dish. Discard the thyme.

Squeeze the flesh from each roasted
garlic clove and mix with any pan
juices. Add the vinegar and mix again.
Pour the mixture over the salad, toss
gently and serve.

Serves 4

Fennel and crispy prosciutto salad

Sherry vinegar dressing
2 tablespoons sherry vinegar
3 tablespoons olive oil

2 small fennel bulbs
2 Lebanese (short) cucumbers
100 g (3 oz/³⁄₄ cup) small black olives
6 slices of prosciutto, chopped
1 handful mint leaves

First, make dressing. Whisk vinegar and oil in a small bowl and season with a little salt and black pepper. Set aside. Next, prepare fennel. Slice off and discard the feathery fronds and stalks from the top of bulbs. Discard the outer layer from each fennel bulb, then cut a thin slice from bottom of each bulb to form a flat base. Sit the fennel upright on a chopping board and slice it very thinly. Transfer slices to a bowl and pour over two-thirds of the dressing. Toss well and then leave to marinate for around 2 hours, or up to 4 hours.

Slice cucumbers in half lengthways and scoop out the seeds using a teaspoon. Chop again at about 1 cm (½ inch) intervals and put cucumber slices in a serving dish with the olives.

Put a frying pan over high heat. When the pan is hot, add the prosciutto and dry-fry until crispy, about 2 minutes. Remove from the pan, leave to cool a little and cut into strips.

Add fennel with all its marinade to the cucumber and olives. Pour over the remaining dressing and toss well. Top with crispy prosciutto and mint leaves and serve.

Serves 4

Chargrilled chicken and sprout salad

600 g (1 lb 5 oz) chicken breast fillets
1 tablespoon olive oil
1 teaspoon ground cumin
1 teaspoon ground coriander
1 tablespoon lemon juice
1 cos (romaine) lettuce, leaves roughly torn
50 g (2 oz) snow pea (mangetout) sprouts, white ends trimmed

Yoghurt and caper dressing
200 g (7 oz) low-fat, thick plain yoghurt
2 tablespoons capers, rinsed, drained and chopped
80 ml (3 fl oz/⅓ cup) lemon juice

Put the chicken breasts in a shallow, non-metallic dish. In a small bowl, mix together the oil, cumin, coriander and lemon juice. Pour the mixture all over the chicken, rubbing it in thoroughly to coat all sides. Cover and leave to marinate in the fridge for 1 hour, or up to 8 hours.

Nearer to serving time, make the yoghurt and caper dressing. Put all the ingredients in a small bowl and add a few grinds of black pepper and 1–2 tablespoons of water to thin it slightly. Whisk well and set aside. Heat a barbecue grill or chargrill pan (griddle) to medium. Add the chicken and cook for 6–8 minutes on one side, then turn and cook for a further 4 minutes, or until cooked through. Remove from the heat and leave to cool slightly, then slice into strips.

Put the lettuce and snow pea sprouts in a serving dish and add the sliced chicken. Pour over the dressing, mix gently and serve.

Serves 4

Roasted tomato, bacon and pasta salad

375 g (13 oz) cherry tomatoes
6 garlic cloves, unpeeled
2 tablespoons olive oil
400 g (14 oz) pasta
6 slices (about 125 g/5 oz) of rindless
  smoked bacon
150 g (5 oz) feta cheese, crumbled
80 g (3 oz/½ cup) Kalamata olives
1 large handful shredded basil

Preheat oven to 180°C (350°F/Gas 4). Put tomatoes and garlic in a roasting dish and drizzle with oil. Season, toss lightly to coat and then bake for about 15–20 minutes (reserve the roasting juices from the pan).

Meanwhile, cook the pasta in a large pot of rapidly boiling salted water until al dente. Drain well.

Put a non-stick frying pan over high heat. Add the bacon and cook for 4–5 minutes, or until crispy. Remove the bacon with tongs, leaving all the pan juices behind, then chop into strips. Swish some pasta around the frying pan to soak up all pan juices. Season with salt and black pepper if needed, then empty into a serving bowl with rest of the pasta, bacon, roasted tomatoes, feta and olives. Toss gently.

Squeeze garlic cloves from their skins and mix them with the roasted tomato juices. Toss through the pasta, scatter with basil and serve warm.

Serves 4

Chickpea and olive salad

330 g (12 oz/1½ cups) dried
   chickpeas
1 small Lebanese (short) cucumber
2 tomatoes
1 small red onion
3 tablespoons chopped flat-leaf
   (Italian) parsley
60 g (2 oz/½ cup) pitted black olives

Dressing
1 tablespoon lemon juice
3 tablespoons olive oil
1 garlic clove, crushed
1 teaspoon honey

Place the chickpeas in a large bowl
and cover with cold water. Leave to
soak overnight.

Drain chickpeas, place in a saucepan,
cover with fresh water and cook for
25 minutes, or until just tender. Drain
and leave to cool.Cut the cucumber in
half lengthways, scoop out the seeds
and cut into 1 cm (½ inch) slices. Cut
the tomatoes into cubes roughly the
same size as the chickpeas, and finely
chop the onion.

Combine the chickpeas, cucumber,
tomato, onion, parsley and olives in
a serving bowl.

To make the dressing, combine all the
ingredients. Pour over the salad and
toss lightly to combine. Serve at room
temperature.

Serves 6

Prawn and rice noodle salad

250 g (9 oz) rice stick noodles
700 g (1 lb 9 oz) raw prawns (shrimp),
  peeled and deveined, tails intact
1 tablespoon olive oil
1 carrot, finely julienned
1 Lebanese (short) cucumber, seeded
  and julienned
2½ large handfuls coriander (cilantro)
  leaves
80 g (3 oz/½ cup) roasted unsalted
  peanuts, chopped
50 g (2 oz) crisp fried shallots
  (see Note)

Dressing
125 ml (4 fl oz/½ cup) rice vinegar
1 tablespoon grated palm sugar
1 garlic clove, finely chopped
2 red chillies, finely chopped
3 tablespoons fish sauce
3 tablespoons lime juice
2 tablespoons peanut oil

Put noodles in a large heatproof bowl, cover with boiling water and leave to soak for 10 minutes. Drain, rinse under cold water to cool, then drain again. Place in a large serving bowl.

Meanwhile, preheat a barbecue grill or chargrill pan (griddle) to high. Toss the prawns in oil and cook until opaque, about 2–3 minutes. Take them off the heat and toss through noodles with the carrot, cucumber and coriander.

To make dressing, combine vinegar, sugar and garlic in a small saucepan. Bring to the boil, then reduce the heat and simmer for 3 minutes to reduce slightly. Pour into a bowl and add the chilli, fish sauce and lime juice. Slowly whisk in the oil, and season to taste.

Toss the dressing through the salad, scatter with the peanuts and crisp fried shallots and serve.

Serves 4

Note: Crisp fried shallots are red Asian shallot flakes used as a garnish in Southeast Asia. They are available from Asian food stores.

Pumpkin, broccoli and chickpea salad with sweet yoghurt dressing

750 g (10 oz) Jap pumpkin or butternut squash, cut into large pieces
400 g (14 oz) can chickpeas, rinsed and drained
1 tablespoon soya bean oil
3 tablespoons sweet chilli sauce
300 g (11 oz) broccoli, cut into florets and steamed
50 g (2 oz) pepitas/shelled pumpkin seeds
2 tablespoons chopped fresh coriander (cilantro)
2 tablespoons low-fat plain yoghurt

Preheat oven to Gas 6/200°C/400°F. Put the pumpkin and chickpeas into a roasting tin, pour over the combined oil and 2 tablespoons of the sweet chilli sauce and toss to coat. Roast for 40 minutes or until the pumpkin is soft. Transfer to a salad bowl and fold through the cooked broccoli, pepitas and coriander.

Whisk together yoghurt and remaining sweet chilli sauce. Drizzle this mixture over salad and toss to combine.

Serves 4

Summer salad of mixed salad greens, mango, avocado and prawns

Dressing
80 ml (3 fl oz/⅓ cup) olive oil
1 tablespoon white wine vinegar
1 tablespoon Dijon mustard
1 teaspoon orange zest, grated

24 (about 600 g/1 lb 5 oz) raw
   medium prawns (shrimp), peeled
   and deveined, tails intact
1 small red onion
2 avocados
2 mangoes
1 baby cos (romaine) lettuce
½ red oakleaf lettuce
½ butter lettuce

To make the dressing, put the olive oil, vinegar, mustard and orange zest in a small bowl and mix well. Season with salt and freshly ground black pepper, to taste.

Preheat a barbecue or chargrill pan to medium heat. Brush prawns with a little of the dressing, arrange on grill plate or pan and cook for 5 minutes, or until crisp and opaque. Transfer to a large bowl.

Finely slice the onion lengthways and add to the bowl. Slice the avocados into large wedges and add to bowl. Slice the cheeks off the mangoes and peel them. Cut into slices and add to the bowl.

Discard damaged outer leaves of the lettuces and tear leaves into smaller pieces. Add to bowl. Pour in dressing and toss lightly before serving.

Serves 4

Eggplant salad with prosciutto

Dressing
2 tablespoons olive oil
1½ tablespoons hazelnut oil
1 tablespoon Spanish sherry vinegar
2 cloves garlic, bruised

2 small (300 g/11 oz each) eggplants (aubergines)
170 ml (6 fl oz/⅔ cup) olive oil
½ bunch red coral lettuce
1 small handful opal (purple) basil
250 g (9 oz) yellow cherry tomatoes
100 g (4 oz) prosciutto, sliced

To make dressing, combine olive oil, hazelnut oil, vinegar and garlic in a small bowl and mix well to combine. Season with salt and freshly ground black pepper, to taste. Set aside for 1 hour to infuse. Discard garlic cloves.

Slice eggplant lengthways into 1.5 cm (⅝ inch) slices, discarding the outer slices that have skin on one face. Put in a colander and then sprinkle with 2–3 teaspoons salt. Set aside to drain in the sink for 30 minutes. Rinse and dry with paper towels.

Heat half the olive oil in a frying pan over medium heat. Fry the eggplant, in batches, for 7–8 minutes, or until lightly brown but tender, adding more oil as required. Drain on paper towels.

Tear the lettuce into large bite-sized pieces and spread them in a shallow serving dish. Add the eggplant slices, basil and whole cherry tomatoes and toss lightly. Clump prosciutto slices into loose bundles and mix between the other ingredients. Drizzle with the dressing just before serving.

Serves 4

Squid salad

Lime and ginger dressing
2 large garlic cloves, crushed
2 teaspoons grated ginger
3 small red chillies, seeded and thinly
  sliced
2 tablespoons grated palm sugar or
  soft brown sugar
2 tablespoons fish sauce
2 tablespoons lime juice

$1/2$ teaspoon sesame oil
500 g (1 lb 2 oz) cleaned squid tubes
6 makrut (kaffir lime) leaves
1 stem lemongrass, white part only,
  chopped
3–4 red Asian shallots, thinly sliced
1 Lebanese (short) cucumber, cut in
  half lengthways, seeded and thinly
  sliced
3 tablespoons chopped coriander
  (cilantro) leaves
1 handful mint leaves
fried red Asian shallot flakes,
  to serve

Put dressing ingredients in a small pan with 1 tablespoon of water. Stir over low heat until the sugar has dissolved. Set aside.

Cut squid tubes in half lengthways and rinse under running water. Score a criss-cross pattern on the inside of the squid, taking care not to cut all the way through, then cut the squid into 3 cm (1$1/4$ inch) pieces.

Put lime leaves and lemongrass in a pot with 1.25 litres (44 fl oz/5 cups) water. Bring to the boil, reduce heat and simmer for 5 minutes. Add half the squid and cook for 30 seconds, or until they begin to curl up and turn opaque. Remove with a slotted spoon and keep warm. Repeat with the rest of the squid, then discard liquid, lime leaves and lemongrass.

Put squid, shallot, cucumber, mint and coriander in a large bowl, add the dressing and toss well. Scatter with fried shallot flakes and serve.

Serves 4

Cannellini bean, capsicum and rocket salad

3 red capsicums (peppers)
1 garlic clove, crushed
zest of 1 lemon
1 large handful flat-leaf parsley,
  coarsely chopped
400 g (14 oz) cooked cannellini or
  flageolet beans
2 tablespoons lemon juice
80 ml (3 fl oz) extra virgin olive oil
100 g (3½ oz) rocket or mixed salad
  leaves

Grill capsicums (peppers) until black, and place in a sealed plastic bag to cool. Remove skin and seeds, then cut into strips. Combine garlic with lemon zest and parsley. Combine rinsed cannellini or flageolet beans with 1 tablespoon lemon juice, half the parsley mixture, 2 tablespoons extra virgin olive oil and salt and pepper to taste. Place the rocket or the salad leaves on a large plate and mix with remaining lemon juice and olive oil.

Scatter the beans over the leaves, then lay pepper strips on top, along with the remaining parsley mixture. Season with salt and pepper and serve immediately.

Serves 4

Note: You can use a 400 g (14 oz) can of beans, rinsed and drained, or soak 250 g (9 oz) dried beans overnight, then boil with a dash of oil and no salt for 30–40 minutes, until tender.

Chargrilled tuna and ruby grapefruit salad

4 ruby grapefruit
cooking oil spray
3 tuna steaks
150 g (5 oz) rocket (arugula) leaves
1 red onion, sliced

Almond and raspberry dressing
2 tablespoons almond oil
2 tablespoons raspberry vinegar
1/2 teaspoon sugar
1 tablespoon shredded mint

Cut a slice off each end of grapefruit and peel away skin, removing all the pith. Separate the segments and set aside in a bowl. Heat a chargrill plate and spray lightly with oil. Cook each tuna steak for 3–4 minutes on each side. This will leave the centre slightly pink. Cool, then thinly slice or flake.

To make dressing, put almond oil, vinegar, sugar and mint in a small screw-top jar and shake until well combined.

Place rocket on a serving plate and top with grapefruit segments, then the tuna and onion. Drizzle with dressing and serve.

Serves 6

Green lentil and ricotta salad

100 g (4 oz) green or puy lentils
3 tablespoons extra virgin olive oil
1 clove garlic, unpeeled
3 tablespoons lemon juice or red
   wine vinegar
2 tablespoons basil, mint or parsley
2 large red capsicums (peppers),
   grilled, skinned and deseeded and
   cut into strips
100 g (4 oz) salad of watercress and
   spinach
100 g (4 oz) low-fat ricotta
25 cm (10 inch) stick crusty French
   bread

Place lentils in a saucepan of water with a dash of olive oil and unpeeled garlic. Bring to the boil and simmer for 30 minutes until just soft. Drain well, remove the skin from the garlic and mix the lentils in a bowl, smashing the garlic to flavour them. Season with 1 tablespoon olive oil and lemon juice.

Purée or chop herbs with remaining 2 tablespoons of olive oil and lemon juice. Season with salt and pepper to taste. Place salad on individual plates, scatter over lentils, divide the pepper strips between plates and spoon over dollops of ricotta. Just before serving, drizzle over the herbs and oil mixture. Serve with crusty French bread.

Serves 4

Sardines with Caesar salad

Dressing
1 egg
2 cloves garlic
2 tablespoons lemon juice
1/2 teaspoon Worcestershire sauce
3–4 anchovy fillets
125 ml (4 fl oz/1/2 cup) extra virgin
  olive oil

100 g (4 oz/1 cup) dry breadcrumbs
65 g (2 oz/2/3 cup) grated parmesan
  cheese
2 tablespoons chopped flat-leaf
  (Italian) parsley
2 eggs, lightly beaten
80 ml (3 fl oz/1/3 cup) milk
16 sardines, scaled and butterflied
oil for deep-frying
12 small poppadoms
2 baby cos (romaine) lettuce, leaves
  separated
8 slices prosciutto, cooked until crisp,
  then broken into pieces
50 g (2 oz) parmesan cheese, shaved

To make dressing, put the egg in a food processor, add the garlic, lemon juice, the Worcestershire sauce and anchovies and process to combine. With the motor running, add the oil in a thin, steady stream until dressing has thickened slightly. Set aside.

Put breadcrumbs, grated parmesan and parsley in a bowl and mix well. Put beaten eggs and milk in another bowl and whisk well. Dip the sardines into the egg wash, then into crumb mixture, and put on a paper-lined baking tray. Refrigerate for 1 hour.

Heat the oil in a deep-fryer or heavy-based frying pan to 180°C (350°F), or until a cube of white bread dropped into oil browns in 15 seconds. Deep-fry poppadoms until crisp, drain on paper towels, then break into pieces. Deep-fry sardines in batches until crisp and golden. Arrange the lettuce, prosciutto, poppadoms and shaved parmesan on serving plates, drizzle with dressing, then top with sardines.

Serves 4

Note: You can use small herring or mackerel as a fish substitution.

Tofu salad

2 teaspoons Thai sweet chilli sauce
1/2 teaspoon grated fresh ginger
1 garlic clove, crushed
2 teaspoons soy sauce
2 tablespoons oil
250 g (9 oz) firm tofu
100 g (4 oz) snow peas (mangetout)
2 small carrots
100 g (4 oz) red cabbage
2 tablespoons chopped peanuts

Combine chilli sauce, ginger, garlic, soy sauce and oil. Cut the tofu into 2 cm (3/4 inch) cubes. Place the tofu in a bowl, pour the marinade over and stir. Cover with plastic wrap and then refrigerate for 1 hour.

Slice snow peas into 3 cm (1 1/4 inch) lengths). Put them in a saucepan, pour boiling water over and leave to stand for 1 minute, then drain and transfer to iced water. Drain well. Cut carrots into batons and finely shred the cabbage.

Add snow peas, carrots and cabbage to tofu and toss lightly to combine. Transfer to a serving bowl or individual plates, sprinkle with peanuts and then serve immediately.

Serves 4

Beetroot and blood orange salad

100 g (4 oz/²/₃ cup) brazil nuts (or
  walnuts)
100 g (4 oz) watercress, spinach and
  beetroot leaves
250 g (9 oz) medium beetroot,
  cooked and peeled
2 oranges
1 tablespoon walnut or sesame oil
1 tablespoon lemon juice or balsamic
  vinegar

Preheat oven to 180°C (350°F/Gas 4). Put the brazil nuts onto a baking tray and roast for 10 minutes. Allow to cool, then coarsely chop. Wash and spin the salad leaves, then arrange on a large plate.

Thinly slice beetroot and pile on top of the salad. Remove skin and pith from the oranges and cut segments into a bowl. Pour remaining juice into bowl, add the walnut oil, olive oil and lemon juice or balsamic vinegar and whisk to combine. Season with salt and black pepper to taste.

Drizzle dressing over the salad and scatter the nuts over the top. Serve immediately.

Serves 4

Wild rice, borlotti bean and bacon salad

100 g (4 oz) borlotti beans, soaked
in cold water overnight
4 cloves garlic, finely chopped
bay leaf
3 tablespoons olive oil
100 g (4 oz/$\frac{1}{2}$ cup) wild rice or half
basmati and half wild rice
1 small onion, finely chopped
100 g (4 oz) pancetta or smoked
bacon,chopped
1 tablespoon chopped fresh sage
25 g (1 oz) dried figs, coarsely
chopped
100 g (4 oz/1 cup) pecans, lightly
toasted, or cashew nuts

Rinse and drain the beans. Put them into a large saucepan of cold water and bring to the boil.Cook, skimming any white foam from the surface. Add 2 cloves of the garlic, the bay leaf and a tablespoon of olive oil and cook for 45 minutes or until the beans are soft. Drain well.

Cook the rice in a large pan of lightly salted water for 40 minutes or until soft, then drain well. Heat remaining oil in a frying pan, add the onion and pancetta and cook over a medium heat for 5 minutes or until the onion is soft and the pancetta is browned.

Add the sage, figs and the remaining chopped cloves of garlic, then cook for 5 minutes, stirring periodically. Stir in the beans, rice and pecans, season to taste with salt and pepper.

Serves 4

Smoked cod and lentil salad

250 g (9 oz/1$\frac{1}{3}$ cups) brown lentils
1 onion, finely chopped
1 bay leaf
500 g (1 lb/2 oz) smoked cod
$\frac{1}{4}$ cup (15 g/$\frac{1}{2}$ oz) chopped fresh dill
3 tablespoons (scallions), chopped
100 g (4 oz) sweet spiced gherkins,
    chopped
100 g (4 oz) sun-dried capsicum,
    chopped

Dressing
2 cloves garlic, crushed
2 tablespoons low-fat mayonnaise
3 tablespoons low-fat plain yoghurt
2 tablespoons chopped chives

Place the lentils, onion and bay leaf in a pan, cover with water and bring to the boil. Reduce the heat and simmer for 25–30 minutes, or until the lentils are just tender. Drain and set aside to cool. Do not overcook the lentils or they will become mushy.

Half-fill a frying pan with water. Bring to the boil and add the smoked cod. Reduce the heat and simmer gently for 10 minutes, or until it flakes when tested with a fork. Drain and allow to cool slightly. Break into large pieces. Add the dill, spring onion, gherkin and capsicum to lentils, then gently fold in the cod pieces.

To make the dressing, combine all the ingredients in a bowl and whisk until smooth. Pour over salad and lightly toss to coat.

Serves 6

Note: Smoked cod is available from most supermarkets or fish markets. You can make this salad up to 3 hours ahead but don't add dressing until you are ready to serve.

Snap pea, carrot and cashew nut salad

100 g (4 oz/^{2}/$_3$ cups) cashews
175 g (6 oz) snap peas or snow peas (mangetout)
125 g (5 oz) carrots
150 g (5 oz) red cabbage

Dressing
3 tablespoons sesame oil
2 tablespoons sunflower oil
2 tablespoons rice wine vinegar or white wine vinegar
1 teaspoon grated or finely chopped ginger
1 tablespoon tamari or light soy sauce

Preheat oven to Gas 6/200°C/400°F. Put cashews on a baking tray and toast for 5 minutes or until golden brown. Allow to cool, then coarsely chop the nuts.

Slice the snap peas or snow peas (mangetout) in half at an angle. Steam or microwave snap peas for 1 minute. Remove them and then leave to cool down. Next, peel the carrot into thin ribbons and finely shred red cabbage.

To make dressing, put the oil, vinegar, ginger and tamari or soy sauce into a salad bowl and whisk to combine. Add vegetables and half the cashews to dressing and toss to coat. Scatter the remaining cashews on the salad.

Serves 4

Niçoise salad

3 eggs
3 tablespoons olive oil
1 tablespoons white wine vinegar
1 small garlic clove, crushed
300 g (11 oz) iceberg lettuce,
  shredded
12 cherry tomatoes, cut into quarters
100 g (4 oz) baby green beans,
  trimmed and blanched
1 small red capsicum (pepper),
  seeded and thinly sliced
1 celery stalk, cut into 5 cm (2 inch)
  strips
1 Lebanese (short) cucumber,
  seeded, cut into 5 cm (2 inch) strips
375 g (13 oz) tin tuna in spring water,
  drained and flaked
12 pitted Kalamata olives, halved
4 anchovy fillets, finely chopped,
  optional

Put eggs in a saucepan of cold water.
Bring slowly to the boil, then reduce
the heat and simmer for 10 minutes.
Stir water during the first few minutes
to centre the yolk. Drain and cool
under cold water, then peel and cut
into quarters.

Combine oil, vinegar and garlic in a
small bowl and mix well. Put lettuce,
tomato, beans, capsicum, celery, the
cucumber, tuna, olives and anchovies
in a large bowl. Pour over dressing
and toss well to combine. Top salad
with the egg quarters and serve with
some crusty wholegrain bread.

Serves 4

Chickpea and parsley salad

440 g (15 oz) tin chickpeas
3 large tomatoes
2 tablespoons chopped parsley
2 teaspoons chopped mint
2 tablespoons lemon juice
2½ tablespoons low-fat plain yoghurt

Drain the chickpeas, rinse under cold running water and drain again. Chop tomatoes into 1 cm (½ inch) pieces and put in a bowl with the drained chickpeas, parsley and the mint. In a small bowl, combine the lemon juice and yoghurt. Pour over the salad and mix until well combined.

Serves 6

Marinated capsicums

3 red capsicums (peppers)
3 sprigs thyme
1 clove garlic, thinly sliced
2 tablepoons flat-leaf leaf (Italian)
    parsley, roughly chopped
1 bay leaf
1 spring onion (scallion), sliced
1 teaspoon paprika
3 tablespoons extra virgin olive oil
2 tablespoons red wine vinegar

Preheat grill (broiler). Cut capsicums (peppers) into quarters, remove the seeds and membrane and grill (broil), skin side up, until the skin blackens and blisters. Cool in a plastic bag, then peel. Slice thinly, then put in a bowl with thyme, thinly sliced garlic clove, parsley, bay leaf and spring onion (scallion). Mix well.

Whisk together the paprika, olive oil, red wine vinegar and salt and freshly ground black pepper. Pour over the capsicum mixture and then toss to combine. Cover and refrigerate for at least 3 hours, or preferably overnight. Remove from the refrigerator about 30 minutes before serving.

Serves 6

Waldorf salad

2 red apples
2 green apples
2 tablespoons lemon juice
$^1/_4$ cup (30 g/1 oz) walnut pieces
250 g (9 oz/1 cup) celery, sliced
3 tablespoons mayonnaise

Quarter apples, remove and discard the seeds and cores, and cut apples into small pieces. Place diced apple in a large bowl, drizzle with the lemon juice and toss to coat (this will prevent the apple discolouring). Add walnut pieces and celery and mix well.

Add mayonnaise to the apple mixture and toss until well coated. Spoon the salad into a lettuce-lined bowl and serve immediately.

Serves 4–6

Note: Waldorf salad can be made up to 2 hours in advance and stored, covered, in refrigerator. It is named after Waldorf-Astoria hotel in New York where it was first served.

Orange and date salad

6 navel oranges
2 teaspoons orange flower water
8 dates, pitted and thinly sliced,
    lengthways
90 g (3 oz/¾ cup) slivered almonds,
    lightly toasted (see Notes)
1 tablespoon shredded mint
¼ teaspoon ras el hanout (see Notes)
    or cinnamon

Peel all the oranges, removing all the pith. Section them by cutting away all the membrane from the flesh. Place the segments in a bowl and squeeze the juice from the remainder of the oranges over them. Add the orange blossom water and stir gently to combine. Cover with plastic wrap and refrigerate until chilled.

Place the orange segments and the juice on a large flat serving dish and scatter the dates and almonds over the top. Sprinkle the mint and ras el hanout over the orange segments. Serve chilled.

Serves 4–6

Notes: Toast the almonds in a dry frying pan over medium heat, stirring constantly, until lightly golden. Watch carefully as they will burn easily. Ras el hanout is a spice mixture commonly used in Morocco.

Somen noodle, prawn and cucumber salad

2 Lebanese (short) cucumbers
1 tablespoon dried wakame seaweed
  pieces
100 g (4 oz) dried somen noodles
12 cooked king prawns (shrimp),
  peeled, deveined and cut in half
  lengthways
3 spring onions (scallions), thinly
  sliced on the diagonal
shichimi togarashi (seven-spice mix),
  to serve, optional

Dressing
½ teaspoon dashi granules
125 ml (4 fl oz/½ cup) Japanese rice
  vinegar
3 tablespoons mirin
1 teaspoon shoyu (Japanese soy
  sauce)
2 teaspoons ginger, very finely grated
pinch sugar
½ teaspoon sesame oil

Cut the cucumbers in half lengthways, scoop out the seeds with a teaspoon, then slice flesh very thinly on a slight diagonal. Put cucumber in a colander, sprinkle with salt and set aside for 10 minutes. Rinse, drain well and then squeeze out as much water as you can. Chill in refrigerator until needed.

Meanwhile, soak the wakame in cold water for 5 minutes, or until glossy and rehydrated, but not mushy. Drain well and chill.

To make the dressing, mix the dashi granules with 1 tablespoon hot water until dissolved. Add rice vinegar, mirin, shoyu, ginger, sugar and sesame oil and stir to combine. Chill.

Bring a large saucepan of water to the boil, then reduce to a simmer. Add the noodles and then cook for 2 minutes, or until tender. Drain and rinse under cold running water until noodles are completely cool. Combine cucumber, wakame, noodles, prawns and half the spring onion in a large bowl. Pour over the dressing and toss well. Serve immediately, garnished with the rest of the spring onion and sprinkle with shichimi togarashi.

Serves 4

Prawn, pawpaw and chilli salad

3 tablespoons olive oil
3 tablespoons lime juice
1 tablespoon fish sauce
2 teaspoons grated palm sugar
1 teaspoon seeded, finely chopped
  red jalapeño chilli
1 teaspoon seeded, finely chopped
  green jalapeño chilli
800 g (1 lb 12 oz) cooked king
  prawns (shrimp)
400 g (14 oz) pawpaw
1 small red onion, finely sliced
2 tablespoons shredded mint
2 tablespoons finely chopped
  coriander

Combine the olive oil, lime juice, fish sauce, palm sugar and chilli in a large mixing bowl and set aside to allow the flavours to combine.

Meanwhile, peel and devein prawns, leaving the tails intact. Peel and discard the seeds from the pawpaw and cut the flesh into bite-sized pieces. Add onion prawns, pawpaw, mint and coriander to the bowl. Very gently, using two spoons, toss the salad to combine. Add the chilli dressing and toss gently again to coat just before serving.

Serves 4

Note: Palm sugar is light brown to very dark brown in colour and is sold in hard cakes for grating. If not available, you can use soft brown sugar instead.

Grilled vegetable salad

1 red onion
6 small eggplants (aubergines), about
   16 cm (6¼ inches) long
4 red capsicums (peppers)
4 orange capsicums (peppers)
1 tablespoon baby capers
80 ml (3 fl oz/⅓ cup) olive oil
1 tablespoon chopped flat-leaf (Italian)
   parsley
2 garlic cloves, finely chopped

Without slicing through the base, cut the onion from top to base into six sections, leaving it attached at base.

Put the onion on a barbecue, or over an open-flamed grill or gas stovetop, with eggplants and capsicums. Cook the vegetables over moderate heat for 10 minutes, turning occasionally, until the eggplants and the capsicum skins are blackened and blistered. Cool the capsicums in a plastic bag for about 10 minutes and set the onion and the eggplant aside. Dry-fry capers with a pinch of salt until crisp. Cut onion into its six sections and discard charred outer skins.

Peel skins off eggplants and remove the stalk. Cut from top to bottom into slices. Peel the capsicums, cut them in half and remove the seeds and membrane. Cut into wide slices.

Arrange all the vegetables on a large serving platter. Drizzle olive oil over them and season well. Scatter the parsley, garlic and capers over top. Serve cold.

Serves 4

Side Salads

Potato salad

600 g (1 lb 5 oz) potatoes, unpeeled,
    cut into bite-sized pieces
1 small onion, finely chopped
1 small green capsicum (pepper),
    chopped
2–3 celery sticks, finely chopped
3 tablespoons finely chopped parsley

Dressing
185 g (6 oz/³⁄₄ cup) mayonnaise
1–2 tablespoons vinegar or lemon
    juice
2 tablespoons sour cream

Cook the potatoes in a large pan of boiling water for 5 minutes, or until just tender (pierce with a small sharp knife—if potato comes away easily it is ready). Drain and cool completely.

Combine the onion, capsicum, celery and the parsley (reserving a little for garnishing) with the cooled potato in a large salad bowl.

To make dressing, mix together the mayonnaise, vinegar and sour cream. Season with salt and pepper. Pour over the salad and then toss gently to combine, without breaking the potato. Garnish with the remaining parsley.

Serves 4

Note: Any potato is suitable for this recipe. Most potatoes are delicious with their skins left on.

Rocket and pecorino salad

3 tablespoons extra virgin olive oil
2 tablespoons lemon juice
150 g (5 oz) rocket (arugula) leaves
pecorino cheese, to serve

Combine the oil with the lemon juice and salt and pepper in a bowl. Add the rocket leaves and toss lightly to coat. Place in a serving dish.

Using a vegetable peeler, shave thin curls of pecorino over salad. Adjust the seasoning and serve.

Serves 4

Mediterranean potato salad

2 eggs
125 g (5 oz) green beans, trimmed
  and cut into 3 cm (1¼ inch)
  lengths
300 g (11 oz) waxy potatoes
100 g (4 oz) penne, fusilli
  or other pasta
2 firm, ripe tomatoes, seeded and
  diced
40 g (1½ oz/¼ cup) Kalamata olives

Anchovy dressing
3 tablespoons olive oil
1 tablespoon white wine vinegar
1 garlic clove, crushed
2 anchovy fillets, finely chopped

Bring a small saucepan of water to the boil. Add the eggs and cook for 7 minutes. Add the green beans and cook for a further 2 minutes. Drain the eggs and beans and rinse under cold water. Leave to cool completely.

Meanwhile, put the potatoes in a pot of salted water and bring to the boil. Cook for about 12 minutes, or until the potatoes are tender when pierced with the tip of a sharp knife. Leave to cool slightly, then cut the potatoes into chunks and place in a large bowl. Bring a separate pot of salted water to the boil and cook pasta until al dente. Drain well, add to potatoes.

To make anchovy dressing, whisk the oil and vinegar in a small bowl until well combined. Stir in the garlic and season with black pepper. Mash the anchovy into dressing, mixing well. Pour dressing over the potatoes and pasta while they are still warm and toss gently.

Peel the eggs and chop them into quarters. Add to the pasta with the beans, tomato and olives. Mix gently and leave to cool completely, then divide the salad between two plates.

Serves 2

Beetroot and chive salad

12 baby beetroot
2 tablespoons pine nuts or pistachio
  nuts
30 g (1 oz/1 cup) picked watercress
  leaves
1 tablespoon snipped chives

Dressing
¼ teaspoon honey
¼ teaspoon Dijon mustard
3 teaspoons balsamic vinegar
1½ tablespoons olive oil

Preheat oven to 200°C (400°F/Gas 6). Trim beetroot bulbs and scrub them well. Put in a roasting dish, cover with foil and roast for 1 hour, or until they are tender. Remove from oven and leave to cool.

Turn oven down to 180°C (350°F/Gas 4). Spread the nuts on a baking tray and bake for 5 minutes, or until lightly golden, ensuring they don't burn. Remove from oven, leave to cool, then roughly chop.

To make dressing, combine honey, mustard and vinegar in a small jug. Whisk in the oil with a fork until well combined, then season to taste. Peel the beetroot, wearing gloves, and halve any larger ones. Divide between two plates along with the watercress and chives, and scatter with the nuts. Drizzle the dressing over the salads just before serving.

Serves 2

Lemon, parsley and onion salad

6 lemons
1 small red onion
2 large handfuls flat-leaf (Italian)
  parsley, chopped
1 teaspoon salt
1 teaspoon caster (superfine) sugar

Peel the lemons with a sharp knife, making sure that all the pith and fine membranes are removed, to expose the flesh. Cut the lemons into 1 cm (1/2 inch) thick slices and remove the seeds. Dice the lemon slices and put them in a bowl.

Halve onion, then slice it thinly. Add the onion and parsley to the lemons, along with the salt and sugar. Toss and set aside for 10 minutes. Just before serving, add a light sprinkling of freshly ground black pepper.

Serves 6–8

Herb salad

100 g (4 oz) baby rocket
  (arugula) leaves
100 g (4 oz) baby English spinach
  leaves
1 small handful basil leaves
1 large handful flat-leaf (Italian)
  parsley, chopped
1 large handful coriander (cilantro)
  leaves, chopped

Dressing
2 tablespoons olive oil
1 tablespoon lemon juice
1 garlic clove, crushed
1 teaspoon honey

Combine the rocket and spinach
leaves with the basil, parsley and
coriander in a bowl.

To make dressing, combine the oil
and lemon with the garlic and honey.
Drizzle over the dressing. Toss well
and serve immediately with freshly
cracked black pepper.

Serves 4

Snow pea salad

200 g (7 oz) snow peas (mangetout)
1 large red capsicum (pepper)
4 oakleaf lettuce leaves
5 green coral lettuce leaves
250 g (9 oz) cherry tomatoes
60 g (2 oz/2 cups) watercress sprigs
parmesan cheese shavings, to serve
  (see Note)

Garlic croutons
3 slices white bread
60 ml (2 fl oz/¼ cup) olive oil
1 garlic clove, crushed

Dressing
2 tablespoons olive oil
1 tablespoon mayonnaise
1 tablespoon sour cream
2 tablespoons lemon juice
1 teaspoon soft brown sugar

Slice the snow peas diagonally. Cut red capsicum in half, remove seeds and membrane and slice.Combine snow peas, red capsicum, lettuces, tomatoes and watercress in a bowl.

To make the croutons, remove the crusts from the bread and discard them. Cut bread into 1 cm (½ inch) squares. Heat the olive oil in a small, heavy-based frying pan and add the crushed garlic. Stir in bread cubes and then cook until golden and crisp. Remove from the heat and leave to drain well on paper towels.

To make dressing, whisk ingredients together with some cracked black pepper in a small bowl for 2 minutes, or until combined. Before serving, top with croutons and parmesan shavings then pour the dressing over the salad, stirring until well combined.

Serves 4–6

Note: Use a vegetable peeler to make thin shavings of parmesan.

Lemon, fennel and rocket salad

2 lemons
2 oranges
1 large fennel bulb or 2 baby fennel
200 g (7 oz) rocket (arugula)
100 g (4 oz/1 cup) pecans, chopped
85 g (3 oz/¼ cup) stuffed green
    olives, halved lengthways

Toasted sesame dressing
1 tablespoon sesame oil
1 tablespoon sesame seeds
3 tablespoons olive oil
2 tablespoons white wine vinegar
1 teaspoon French mustard

Peel lemons and oranges, removing all the white pith. Cut the fruit into thin slices and remove any seeds. Thinly slice fennel. Wash and dry the rocket leaves and tear into pieces. Chill the salad while making the dressing.

To make the dressing, heat the oil in a small pan over moderate heat. Add the sesame seeds and fry, stirring constantly, until lightly golden.

Remove from the heat and cool. Pour the mixture into a small jug, whisk in the remaining ingredients and season with salt and ground black pepper. Combine fruit, fennel, rocket, pecans and olives in a shallow serving bowl. Drizzle with the dressing.

Note: Blood oranges have a lovely tart flavour and, when in season, are delicious in this recipe.

Serves 4

Leek and caper salad

5 leeks, white part only
80 ml (3 fl oz/⅓ cup) olive oil
2 tablespoons sherry vinegar
2 tablespoons baby capers, rinsed

Cut the leeks in half lengthways and wash under cold running water. Cut them into 5 cm (2 inch) lengths, then cut in half again lengthways. Heat the oil in a large heavy-based pan, add the leeks and stir until coated with the oil. Cover and cook over low heat for 15–20 minutes, or until the leeks are soft and tender (but don't let them brown or burn). Cool for 10 minutes.

Stir through the vinegar and season to taste with salt and pepper. Transfer to a serving dish and scatter with baby capers (if baby capers are unavailable, use chopped ordinary-sized capers).

Serves 6

Chargrilled tomato salad

8 Roma (plum) tomatoes
1½ teaspoon capers, rinsed and
   drained
4 basil leaves, torn
3 teaspoons olive oil
3 teaspoons balsamic vinegar
1 garlic clove, crushed
¼ teaspoon honey

Cut the tomatoes lengthways into quarters and scoop out seeds. Heat a chargrill pan (griddle) to medium and cook tomato quarters for 1–2 minutes on each side, or until grill marks appear and tomatoes have softened. Cool to room temperature and place in a bowl.

Combine capers, basil, oil, vinegar, garlic and honey in a small bowl and season with salt and freshly ground black pepper. Pour the mixture over the tomatoes and then toss together gently. Serve at room temperature with crusty bread and grilled meats.

Serves 4

Broad bean rotollo with salad greens

Rotollo
750 g (1 lb 10 oz) broad (fava) beans,
  shelled to give 275 g
  (10 oz/1½ cups)
4 eggs
4 egg yolks
2 teaspoons mint, finely chopped
2 teaspoons basil, finely chopped
20 g (1 oz) butter
80 g (3 oz) pecorino cheese, grated

Salad
1½ tablespoons pine nuts
1 tablespoon basil, chopped
80 ml (3 fl oz/⅓ cup) olive oil
2 tablespoons lemon juice
2 baby cos (romaine) lettuces,
  trimmed
2 witlof (chicory/Belgian endive),
  preferably purple, trimmed

To make rotollo, bring a saucepan of water to the boil. Add a large pinch of salt and broad beans and simmer for 2 minutes. Drain and peel skins.

Preheat the oven to 160°C (315°F/ Gas 2–3). Beat eggs, mint and basil together and season. Melt half the butter in a 20 cm (8 inch) frying over medium heat. Pour in half the egg mixture and cook until base has set but top is still a little runny.

Slide omelette from pan onto a sheet of baking paper. Scatter half of the pecorino and half the broad beans over surface. Roll omelette into a tight sausage. Roll the baking paper around omelette and tie both ends with string to prevent it from unrolling. Put on a baking sheet. Repeat with remaining ingredients. Bake for about 8 minutes. Remove from oven, set aside for 2–3 minutes, unwrap and set aside to cool. Toast pine nuts for 4–5 minutes until golden.

To make salad, put 1 tablespoon of pine nuts, basil, olive oil and lemon juice in a food processor and process until smooth. Put 2 tablespoons of dressing with the leaves. Slice rotollo into and scatter over salad, with pine nuts. Drizzle dressing over the top.

Serves 4

Crunchy cabbage, carrot and almond slaw

115 g (4 oz) finely shredded red
cabbage
115 g (4 oz) finely shredded Chinese
cabbage
2 carrots, cut into thin matchsticks
2 stalks celery, thinly sliced
1 red pepper (capsicum), cut into
thin strips
3 spring onions (scallions), thinly
sliced
75 g (3 oz) flaked almonds, toasted
100 g (4 oz) boiled noodles

Dressing
1 small red chilli, finely chopped
3 tablespoons lime juice
1 tablespoon fish sauce
1 tablespoon sesame oil
1 tablespoon soft brown sugar

Put the cabbages, carrots, celery, red pepper, spring onions and the almonds into a arge salad bowl and toss to combine.

Whisk together the chilli, lime juice, fish sauce, sesame oil and the brown sugar until the sugar dissolves. Pour the dressing over the salad and toss to combine. Allow this to stand for 15 minutes before serving.

Finally, add the noodles and toss quickly before serving immediately.

Serves 4

Tomato, egg and olive salad

6 ripe tomatoes
1 red onion, thinly sliced
6 hard-boiled eggs, peeled and sliced
90 g (3 oz/½ cup) marinated black
  olives
a few torn basil leaves, to serve
extra virgin olive oil, to drizzle

Cut the tomatoes into thick slices and arrange on a large plate. Top with the onion, eggs and olives and scatter the basil leaves over the top.

Drizzle with some extra virgin olive oil and sprinkle generously with sea salt and freshly cracked black pepper.

Serves 4

Herbed pasta and salmon salad

400 g (14 oz) small shell pasta
250 g (9 oz) cherry tomatoes,
  quartered, or halved if small
1 large yellow capsicum (pepper),
  seeded and diced
2 sticks celery, thinly sliced
3 spring onions (scallions), thinly
  sliced
80 g (3 oz/½ cup) pitted green olives
  in brine, drained and chopped
2 tablespoons capers, rinsed and
  chopped, optional
200 g (7 oz) smoked salmon, sliced
1 handful basil, finely shredded
3 tablespoons finely chopped flat-leaf
  (Italian) parsley
125 ml (4 fl oz/½ cup) ready-made
  fat-free Italian salad dressing

Cook pasta in a large saucepan of boiling water for 10 minutes, or until just cooked. Rinse under cold water to cool. Drain. Place in a large bowl.

Place all the other ingredients into the bowl with the pasta, add the dressing and toss together.

Serves 4

Note: Any type of small pasta shapes and fat-free dressing can be used in this recipe.

Sprout and cabbage salad

1/2 small red cabbage
  (600 g/1 lb 5 oz), core removed,
  finely shredded
420 g (15 oz) tin four bean mix,
  drained and rinsed
200 g (7 oz/2¼ cups) mung bean
  sprouts
4 large spring onions (scallions),
  sliced

Dressing
1 tablespoon olive oil
2 teaspoons lemon juice
1 large garlic clove, crushed

Put the shredded cabbage, four bean mix, bean sprouts and spring onions in a serving bowl. Mix together gently.

To make the dressing, whisk the olive oil and the lemon juice together in a small bowl. Stir in the garlic and then season with salt and freshly ground black pepper. Pour dressing over the salad and toss to combine.

Serves 6

White salad

200 g (7 oz) silken firm tofu

Salad
100 g (4 oz) konnyaku (yam cake)
1 small carrot, peeled
170 ml (6 fl oz/²/₃ cup) dashi II
3 teaspoons shoyu (Japanese soy sauce)
1 tablespoon mirin
12 baby green beans, cut into 3 cm (1¼ inch) lengths
6 fresh shiitake mushrooms, stems discarded, caps sliced

Tofu Dressing
50 g (2 oz/¹/₃ cup) sesame seeds, toasted
1 tablespoon caster (superfine) sugar
1 tablespoon white miso paste
½ teaspoon dashi granules
2 teaspoons shoyu (Japanese soy sauce)
3 teaspoons mirin
3 teaspoons sake

To weight tofu, first wrap it in a clean tea towel (dish towel). Put two plates on top of it and leave for 2 hours to extract excess moisture. Meanwhile, prepare salad. Boil the konnyaku for 2 minutes, then cut into 3 cm x 5 mm (1¼ x ¼ inch) strips. Cut carrot into 5 cm (2 inch) long pieces. Slice each piece into 1 cm (½ inch) wide batons.

To make the dashi, dissolve dashi granules in 1½ tablespoons of hot water. Mix dashi, shoyu and mirin in a saucepan and bring to the boil over high heat. Reduce to a simmer, then add konnyaku, carrot and beans and cook for 3 minutes, or until carrot is tender. Remove the vegetables with a slotted spoon and set aside. Add the shiitake to pan, increase heat to high and cook for 1–2 minutes, or until the liquid has almost evaporated. Cool completely. Remove tofu from the tea towel, then pat dry. Mash tofu with the back of a fork and then set aside.

To make the dressing, grind sesame seeds using a mortar and pestle until crushed. Mix in sugar, miso, dashi, shoyu, mirin and sake until smooth. Stir in tofu. Put cooled carrot and shiitake mixture in a bowl along with dressing and toss to combine. Serve in serving bowl or in individual dishes.

Serves 6

Spinach with sesame dressing

200 g (7 oz) English spinach, stems
  trimmed
shoyu (Japanese soy sauce),
  for sprinkling

Dressing
50 g (2 oz/1/3 cup) white or black
  sesame seeds
1 1/2 teaspoons caster (superfine)
  sugar
1 tablespoon sake
1/2 teaspoon dashi granules
2 teaspoons tamari

Rinse spinach thoroughly to remove any grit. Bring a saucepan of salted water to the boil, add spinach and cook for 1 minute. Drain and plunge into iced water to stop the cooking process, then drain well again. Wrap in a bamboo sushi mat or tea towel (dish towel) and squeeze out any excess water. Sprinkle lightly with a little shoyu, allow to cool, then cut into 3 cm (1 1/4 in) lengths and place on a serving platter.

To make the dressing, dry-fry the sesame seeds over medium heat, stirring regularly, for about 5 minutes, or until lightly toasted and aromatic. Immediately scoop into a mortar or a suribachi (Japanese ribbed mortar), reserving 1 teaspoon of whole seeds for garnish, and grind with the pestle until very finely crushed.

Dissolve the dashi garnules in 1 1/2 tablespoons of hot water and then gradually incorporate the sugar, sake, the dashi and the tamari until it forms a smooth paste. Spoon some sesame paste on top of each spinach bundle. Sprinkle with the reserved toasted sesame seeds and serve.

Serves 4–6

Cucumber and olive salad

4 Lebanese (short) cucumbers
1/2 teaspoon salt
1 red onion, finely chopped
3 teaspoons caster (superfine) sugar
1 tablespoon red wine vinegar
3 tablespoons olive oil
1 teaspoon finely chopped lemon
  thyme
90 g (3 oz/1/2 cup) black olives

Wash cucumbers and dry with paper towels. Do not peel the cucumbers if the skin is tender. Coarsely grate the cucumbers, then mix in the salt and leave to drain well. Add the red onion and sugar and toss together.

In a small bowl beat together the red wine vinegar and olive oil, then add lemon thyme and freshly ground black pepper, to taste. Whisk ingredients together and pour over the cucumber. Cover and then chill for 15 minutes. Scatter with the olives and serve with flat bread.

Serves 4

Preserved lemon
and tomato salad

750 g (1 lb 10 oz) tomatoes
1 red onion
1 preserved lemon
3 tablespoons olive oil
1 tablespoon lemon juice
1/2 teaspoon paprika
1 tablespoon flat-leaf (Italian) parsley,
   finely chopped
2 tablespoons coriander (cilantro)
   leaves, finely chopped

Peel tomatoes. To do this, score a cross in the base of each one using a knife. Put the tomatoes in a bowl of boiling water for 20 seconds, then plunge them into a bowl of cold water to cool. Remove from water and peel skin away from the cross — it should slip off easily. Cut the tomatoes in half horizontally and squeeze out seeds. Dice the tomatoes and put them in a bowl. Halve the onion lengthways, cut out the root end and slice into slender wedges and add to the bowl.

Separate the preserved lemon into quarters, remove pulp and membrane and discard them. Rinse the rind, pat dry with paper towels and cut into fine strips. Add to the onion and tomato.

Beat together the olive oil, lemon juice and the paprika, and add 1/2 teaspoon salt and black pepper. Pour over the salad, toss lightly, then cover and set aside for 30 minutes. Just before serving, add parsley and coriander and toss again.

Serves 4

Beetroot and cumin salad

6 medium-sized beetroots
80 ml (3 fl oz/⅓ cup) olive oil
1 tablespoon red wine vinegar
½ teaspoon ground cumin
1 red onion
2 tablespoons flat-leaf (Italian) parsley, chopped

Cut stems from the beetroots, leaving 2 cm (¾ inch) attached. Do not trim the roots. Wash them well to remove all traces of soil, then boil in salted water for 1 hour, or until tender.

Meanwhile, to make the dressing combine the olive oil, red wine vinegar and cumin in a deep bowl with a good grinding of black pepper and whisk.

Wearing rubber gloves so beetroot juice doesn't stain your hands, peel the warm beetroot bulbs and trim the roots. Halve them and cut into slender wedges and place in dressing. Halve the onion, slice it into slender wedges and add to the beetroot. Add parsley and toss well. Serve warm or at room temperature.

Serves 4–6

Main Courses

Chilli chicken and cashew salad

2 teaspoons olive oil
300 g (11 oz) chicken breast fillets
50 g (2 oz) salad leaves
125 g (5 oz) cherry tomatoes, halved
1/2 Lebanese (short) cucumber, cut
    into bite-sized chunks
50 g (2 oz) snow pea (mangetout)
    sprouts, trimmed
40 g (1 1/2 oz/1/4 cup) cashew nuts,
    roughly chopped

Dressing
1 1/2 tablespoons Thai sweet chilli
    sauce
1 tablespoon lime juice
1 teaspoon fish sauce
1 tablepoon chopped coriander
    (cilantro)
1 small garlic clove, crushed
1/2 small red chilli, finely chopped
1 teaspoon grated ginger
2 teaspoons peanut or sesame oil

Heat oil in a frying pan or chargrill pan (griddle). Add chicken and cook over medium heat for 5–8 minutes on each side, or until cooked through. While still hot, slice each breast widthways into strips.

Combine the dressing ingredients in a large bowl and mix well. Toss the warm chicken strips through the dressing and leave to cool slightly.

Divide the salad leaves, the tomato, cucumber and the snow pea sprouts between two plates and scatter with the cashews. Drizzle the dressing over the salads and serve.

Serves 2

Chicken with mixed rice, sultanas and toasted cashews

140 g (5 oz/^{2}/$_3$ cup) mixed rice blend
(see Note)
50 g (2 oz/^{1}/$_3$ cup) cashew nuts
100 g (4 oz) shredded roasted
or barbecued chicken
40 g (1^1/$_2$ oz/^{1}/$_3$ cup) sultanas
8–10 coriander (cilantro) sprigs

Coriander dressing
2 tablespoons olive oil
1 tablepoon red wine vinegar
1 teaspoon seeded mustard
2 tablespoons finely chopped
coriander (cilantro) leaves

Cook the rice according to the packet instructions, then drain well. Rinse under cold water and drain well again. Fluff up with a fork to separate grains, then leave to cool in a sieve.

While the rice is cooling, put a frying pan over high heat. Add the cashews and dry-fry for 1–2 minutes, tossing them about so they colour evenly. When the nuts are lightly toasted, put them on a chopping board, leave to cool, then roughly chop them.

Put all dressing ingredients, except the coriander leaves, in a small bowl and then whisk until well combined. Season lightly with salt and black pepper, then stir in the coriander.

When the rice is cold, mix through the shredded chicken, the cashews and sultanas. Stir in dressing, season with salt and pepper and mix well. Divide between two plates and scatter with coriander sprigs.

Serves 2

Note: You could also use leftover rice for this recipe. You will need about 350 g (12 oz/2 cups) of cold cooked rice.

Brown rice, tuna and roasted vegetable salad

1 small red capsicum (pepper),
   roughly chopped
1 zucchini (courgette), thickly sliced
1 small onion, cut into wedges
2 tablespoons olive oil
140 g (5 oz/^{2}/$_3$ cup) brown rice (see
   Note)
185 g (7 oz) tin tuna chunks, drained

Orange and basil dressing
zest of 1 orange
2 tablespoons orange juice
2 tablespoons olive oil
3 tablespoons torn basil leaves

Preheat oven to 200°C (400°F/Gas 6). Put the capsicum, zucchini and onion in a baking dish. Pour the oil over the top, season with the salt and pepper, then toss to coat the vegetables with oil. Bake for 20 minutes or until lightly golden and soft, stirring occasionally during cooking.

Meanwhile, cook the rice according to the packet instructions. Drain well, then rinse under cold water and drain again. Leave to cool in a sieve over a saucepan, fluffing up the grains with a fork occasionally.

While the rice is cooling, put all the orange and basil dressing ingredients in a bowl and whisk well. Season with salt and black pepper. Put the cooled rice in a bowl, then stir in the tuna and all the roasted vegetables. Pour over the dressing, gently toss together, and divide salad between two plates.

Serves 2

Note: You could also use leftover rice for this recipe. You will need about 280 g (10 oz/1^1/$_2$ cups) of cold cooked brown rice.

Asian pork salad with ginger and chilli dressing

3 cm (1¼ inch) piece of ginger,
  peeled and julienned
1 teaspoon rice vinegar
½ small red chilli, seeded
  and finely chopped
1 tablespoon light soy sauce
a few drops of sesame oil
½ star anise
1 teaspoon lime juice
125 g (5 oz) Chinese roast pork
  (char siu)
50 g (2 oz) snow pea (mangetout)
  sprouts
2 spring onions (scallions), thinly
  sliced on the diagonal
½ small red capsicum (pepper),
  thinly sliced

To make the ginger and chilli dressing, combine the ginger, vinegar, chilli, soy sauce, sesame oil, star anise and the lime juice in a small saucepan. Gently warm for 2 minutes, or until just about to come to the boil, then set aside to cool. Once it has cooled, remove the star anise.

Thinly slice pork and divide between two plates along with the snow pea sprouts, spring onion and capsicum. Drizzle the dressing over the salad just before serving.

Serves 2

Chicken salad

150 g (5 oz) snow peas (mangetout),
  trimmed
1 tablespoon oil
20 g (1 oz) butter
4 chicken breast fillets
1 carrot, cut into julienne strips
2 celery sticks, cut into julienne strips
3 spring onions (scallions), cut into
  julienne strips
150 g (5 oz) button mushrooms,
  sliced
1 handful flat-leaf parsley, chopped
1 tablespoon chopped tarragon
150 g (5 oz) watercress or baby
  English spinach leaves
2 tablespoons almonds, chopped

Dressing
3 tablespoons extra virgin olive oil
1 tablespoon white wine vinegar
1/2 teaspoon sugar
3 tablespoons mayonnaise
2 tablespoons sour cream
1 tablespoon Dijon mustard

Plunge the snow peas (mangetout)
into a pan of boiling water, return to
the boil and cook for 1 minute, or until
tender but still crisp. Rinse under cold
water and drain well. Cut diagonally
into strips.

Heat the oil and butter in a frying pan,
add chicken and cook for 7 minutes
on each side over medium heat, or
until tender and well browned all over.
Drain on paper towels and allow to
cool. Slice.

Mix the carrot, celery, spring onion,
snow peas, chicken, mushrooms,
parsley and tarragon, and season
with salt and black pepper.

To make the dressing, combine the
oil, vinegar and sugar in a jug. Whisk
until well blended, then season with
salt and freshly ground black pepper.
Add the mayonnaise, sour cream and
mustard and whisk until well blended.
Place watercress in a serving dish,
top with chicken salad, drizzle with
dressing and sprinkle with almonds.

Serves 6

Grilled haloumi salad with herb dressing

1 large Lebanese (short) cucumber, seeded and diced
3 tomatoes, seeded and diced
40 g (1½ oz/¼ cup) pitted and halved Kalamata olives
2 tablespoons capers, rinsed and drained
1 small red onion, finely diced
300 g (11 oz) haloumi cheese, cut into 1 cm (½ inch) slices

Herb dressing
1 garlic clove, roughly chopped
1 small handful basil leaves
1 small handful flat-leaf (Italian) parsley
3 tablespoons olive oil
2 tablespoons lemon juice

Heat a barbecue grill or chargrill pan (griddle) to medium. While heating, prepare salad: simply put cucumber, tomato, olives, capers and onion in a serving dish and mix together gently.

To make herb dressing, crush garlic in a mortar and pestle with a pinch of salt. Add basil and parsley and pound until a paste starts to form. Add a little oil and pound for 10 seconds. Stir in remaining oil and the lemon juice and season with pepper. (If preferred, you can purée the ingredients in a food processor instead.) Set aside.

Grill the haloumi for 1–2 minutes on each side until it is starting to soften but not melt. Cut haloumi into thick strips and arrange on top of salad. Spoon over the dressing and serve at once while haloumi is still hot, before it becomes rubbery and tough.

Serves 4

Spicy pork salad

1 tablespoon oil
500 g (1 lb 2 oz) pork mince
2 tablespoons fish sauce
1 tablespoon soy sauce
2^1/$_2$ tablespoons lime juice
1 tablespoon soft brown sugar
10 spring onions (scallions), finely
    chopped
3 stems lemongrass, white part only,
    finely chopped
2 red chillies, seeded and sliced
2 tablespoons each of chopped fresh
    coriander (cilantro), mint and parsley
lettuce leaves, for serving

Heat oil in a frying pan. Add the mince and cook over medium heat until well browned, breaking up any lumps with a fork as it cooks. Remove from pan and leave to cool.

Combine fish sauce, soy sauce, lime juice and brown sugar in a bowl. Add pork mince. Mix in the spring onion, lemongrass, chilli and herbs. Cover and refrigerate for at least 3 hours, stirring occasionally, or overnight.

To serve, lay a lettuce leaf on each plate and then spoon in some of the pork mixture.

Serves 6

Sausage and egg salad with anchovy dressing

4 eggs
250 g (9 oz) green beans, trimmed
   and halved
2 tablespoons olive oil
4 good quality sausages, cut into
   1 cm (½ inch) slices
2 thick slices crusty white
   bread, crusts removed, cut into
   1 cm (½ inch) cubes
200 g (7 oz) mixed salad leaves
150 g (5 oz) roasted red capsicum
   (pepper), sliced

Anchovy dressing
1 garlic clove, crushed
3 tablespoons olive oil
2 tablespoons lemon juice
3 anchovy fillets, finely chopped
2 tablespoons shredded basil leaves

Bring a small saucepan of water to the boil, add the eggs and cook for 5 minutes. Add the beans and cook for a further 2 minutes. Drain and rinse the eggs and beans under cold water, draining the beans well. Crack egg shells slightly and leave to cool in cold water.

Meanwhile, heat half the oil in a frying pan. Add sausage slices and fry over medium heat for 5 minutes, or until golden and cooked, turning once. Remove from the pan using a slotted spoon and set aside. Put the frying pan back over medium heat and add the remaining oil. When the oil is hot, add the bread cubes and fry, turning now and then, for about 2 minutes, or until golden on all sides.

Put all anchovy dressing ingredients in a small bowl. Mash the anchovies well, mix thoroughly, then season with black pepper and set aside.

Once eggs have cooled, peel them and then cut them into quarters. Put the sausages, beans, the salad leaves and capsicum in a serving bowl. Add the dressing and toss gently. Top with the eggs and croutons and serve.

Serves 4

Seared tuna and white bean salad

400 g (14 oz) fresh tuna steaks
1 small red onion, thinly sliced
1 tomato, seeded and chopped
1 small red capsicum (pepper), thinly
  sliced
2 x 400 g (14 oz) tins cannellini
  beans, rinsed and drained
2 garlic cloves, crushed
1 teaspoon chopped thyme
1 very large handful flat-leaf (Italian)
  parsley, finely chopped
oil, for brushing
100 g (4 oz) baby salad leaves or
  baby rocket (arugula) leaves
1 teaspoon lemon zest strips

Warm vinaigrette
1½ tablespoons lemon juice
80 ml (3 fl oz/⅓ cup) extra virgin olive
  oil
1 teaspoon honey

Put tuna steaks on a plate, sprinkle both sides with plenty of cracked black pepper, cover with plastic wrap and refrigerate until needed. Nearer to serving time, toss onion, tomato and capsicum in a large mixing bowl with the beans, garlic, thyme and parsley.

To make the warm vinaigrette, put oil, lemon juice and honey in a saucepan, bring to the boil, then simmer, stirring, for 1 minute, or until the honey has dissolved. Remove from the heat but keep warm.

Brush a barbecue hotplate or chargrill pan (griddle) with a little oil and heat until very hot. Cook tuna steaks for 1–2 minutes on each side, depending on their thickness — they should still be pink in the middle. Slice into large cubes and add to the beans. Pour the warm dressing over top and toss well.

Divide the beans and tuna between four serving plates. Top with the salad leaves, scatter with the lemon zest and serve.

Serves 4

Broad bean, smoked chicken and pesto salad

Pistachio pesto
1 small handful basil
100 g (4 oz) rocket (arugula) picked
  over to give 30 g (1 oz)
2 tablespoons grated parmesan
  cheese
1 clove garlic
25 g (1 oz/¼ cup) pistachio kernels,
  roasted
3 tablespoons olive oil
2 tablespoons cream (whipping)

700 g (1 lb 9 oz/4 cups) broad (fava)
  beans in the pod, shelled to give
  250 g (9 oz)
1 small smoked chicken
1 bulb fennel (or 2 baby fennel bulbs)
½ small red capsicum (pepper),
  julienned
1 large handful salad greens

To make pesto, put the basil, rocket, parmesan, garlic and pistachios in a small food processor and process until smooth. Add the oil and process until combined. You will only need half the pesto — store remainder for later use. Put half the pesto into a bowl and stir in the cream. Gradually stir in about 1 tablespoon warm water to give a coating consistency. Season with salt and ground black pepper.

Bring a medium saucepan of water to the boil. Add a large pinch of salt and the broad beans and then simmer for 2 minutes. Drain and plunge into iced water. Drain again and peel skins off the beans, discarding skins. Remove the flesh from the chicken and cut it into bite-sized pieces. Very finely slice fennel lengthways. This is best done using a mandolin. Put broad beans, chicken, fennel, red capsicum and the salad greens in a bowl. Add the pesto and toss well to coat. Serve at once.

Serves 4

Roast beef and spinach salad with horseradish cream

Serves 4

Horseradish cream
125 g (5 oz/½ cup) thick plain yoghurt
1 tablepoon creamed horseradish
2 tablespoons lemon juice
2 tablespoons cream
2 garlic cloves, crushed
a few drops of Tabasco sauce,
   or to taste

200 g (7 oz) green beans, trimmed
500 g (1 lb 2 oz) rump steak
1 red onion, halved
1 tablespoon olive oil
100 g (4 oz) baby English spinach
   leaves
50 g (2 oz/1⅔ cups) picked
   watercress leaves
200 g (7 oz/1½ cups) semi-dried
   (sun-blushed) tomatoes

To make horseradish cream, whisk all the ingredients in a small bowl with a little black pepper to taste. Cover and then chill for 15 minutes. Bring a pot of lightly salted water to the boil, add the beans and blanch for 4 minutes, or until tender. Drain, refresh under cold water and drain again.

Meanwhile, preheat a griller (broiler) or barbecue hotplate to high. Brush the steak and onion halves with the oil. Cook the steak for 2 minutes on each side, or until seared but still rare, then remove from the heat, cover with foil and leave for 5 minutes. (Cook beef a little longer if you prefer it medium or well done.) While the steak is resting, cook the onion for 2–3 minutes on each side, or until charred.

Toss the spinach, watercress, tomato and beans in a large salad bowl. Slice the beef thinly across the grain, then layer over the salad. Thinly slice the grilled onion, add to the salad and drizzle with the dressing. Season well with sea salt and freshly ground black pepper and serve.

Spicy lamb and noodle salad

1 tablespoon five-spice powder
3 tablespoons vegetable oil
2 garlic cloves, crushed
2 lamb backstraps or fillets (about
   250 g/9 oz each)
500 g (1 lb 2 oz) fresh Shanghai
   (wheat) noodles
1½ teaspoons sesame oil
80 g (3 oz) snow pea (mangetout)
   sprouts
½ red capsicum (pepper), thinly sliced
4 spring onions (scallions), thinly
   sliced on the diagonal
2 tablespoons sesame seeds, toasted

Dressing
1 tablespoon finely chopped ginger
1 tablespoon Chinese black vinegar
1 tablespoon Chinese rice wine
2 tablespoons peanut oil
2 teaspoons chilli oil

Combine the five-spice powder, 2 tablespoons of vegetable oil and garlic in a large bowl. Add the lamb and turn to coat well. Cover and marinate for 30 minutes.

Cook noodles in a large saucepan of boiling water for 4–5 minutes, or until tender. Drain, rinse with cold water and drain again. Add the sesame oil and toss to combine.

Heat the remaining vegetable oil in a large frying pan. Cook the lamb over medium–high heat for 3 minutes each side for medium–rare, or until cooked to your liking. Rest for 5 minutes, then thinly slice across the grain.

To make dressing, combine ginger, the Chinese black vinegar, rice wine, peanut oil and chilli oil. Place noodles, lamb strips, snow pea sprouts, the spring onion, capsicum and dressing in a large bowl and toss gently until well combined. Sprinkle with sesame seeds and serve.

Serves 4

Lamb, capsicum and cucumber salad

1 red onion, very thinly sliced
1 red capsicum (pepper), very thinly
  sliced
1 green capsicum (pepper), very thinly
  sliced
2 large Lebanese (short) cucumbers,
  cut into batons
2 large handfuls mint, shredded
3 tablespoons chopped dill
3 tablespoons olive oil
600 g (1 lb 5 oz) lamb backstraps
  or fillets
80 ml (2 fl oz/⅓ cup) lemon juice
2 small garlic cloves, crushed
100 ml (4 fl oz) extra virgin olive oil

Combine the onion, red and green capsicums, cucumber, mint and dill in a large bowl.

Heat a chargrill pan or frying pan until hot. Drizzle with the oil and cook the lamb for 2–3 minutes on each side, or until it is tender but still a little pink. Remove from pan and allow to rest for 5 minutes. Thinly slice lamb and add to the salad, tossing to mix.

Combine the lemon juice and garlic in a small jug, then whisk in the extra virgin olive oil with a fork until well combined. Season with salt and black pepper, then gently toss the dressing through the salad.

Serves 4

Note: This salad is delicious served on fresh or toasted Turkish bread spread with hummus.

Chicken and sweet potato salad

4 Roma (plum) tomatoes, quartered
  lengthways
300 g (11 oz) eggplant (aubergine),
  quartered lengthways
oil spray
500 g (1 lb 2 oz) orange sweet
  potato, peeled and cut into
  2 cm (3/4 inch) slices
1 large red onion, sliced into thin
  wedges
1 barbecued chicken
2 tablespoons chopped coriander
  (cilantro) leaves
2–3 tablespoons balsamic vinegar
2 handfuls rocket (arugula)

Preheat oven to 200°C (400°F/Gas 6).
Place the tomatoes and eggplant on
a large, non-stick baking tray, spray
with a little oil and then season with
salt and freshly ground black pepper.
Bake, turning the eggplant halfway
through, for 25–30 minutes.

Meanwhile, steam the sweet potato
for 15 minutes, or until just tender.
Place in a large bowl with the tomato
and eggplant.

Lightly spray a small non-stick frying
pan with oil, add the onion and cook
over a low heat for 6 minutes, or until
golden. Set aside.

Remove the skin and the bones from
chicken and discard. Cut the chicken
meat into bite-sized pieces and add
to vegetables with the coriander and
1 tablespoon balsamic vinegar. Toss
gently to combine.

Place rocket on a platter, then the
chicken mixture and top with onion.
Drizzle with the remaining balsamic
vinegar to taste and serve with thick
slices of wholegrain bread.

Serves 6

Grilled haloumi and roast vegetable salad

4 slender eggplants (aubergines), cut
  in half and then halved lengthways
1 red capsicum (pepper), halved,
  thickly sliced
4 small zucchini (courgette), cut in half
  and then halved lengthways
80 ml ($2^3/_4$ fl oz/$^1/_3$ cup) olive oil
2 cloves garlic, crushed
200 g (7 oz) haloumi cheese, thinly
  sliced
150 g (5 oz) baby English spinach
  leaves, trimmed
1 tablespoon balsamic vinegar

Preheat oven to hot 220°C(425°F/
Gas 7). Place the vegetables in a
large bowl, add 3 tablespoons of the
olive oil and the garlic, season and
toss well to combine.

Place the vegetables in an ovenproof
dish in a single layer. Roast for around
20–30 minutes, or until tender and
browned around the edges.

Meanwhile, cook the haloumi slices
on a hot, lightly oiled barbecue grill
for 1–2 minutes each side.

Top spinach with haloumi and the
roast vegetables. Whisk the rest of
the oil and the vinegar together to
make a dressing.

Serves 4

Minty beef noodle salad

oil spray
500 g (1 lb 2 oz) piece lean beef rump
  steak
250 g (9 oz) dry thin rice vermicelli
  noodles
250 g (9 oz) cherry tomatoes, halved
2 x 100 g (4 oz) packets baby Asian
  salad leaves
1 Lebanese (short) cucumber, peeled,
  seeded and thinly sliced
1/4 red onion, cut into thin slivers
6 radishes, thinly sliced
1 handful mint

Dressing
3 tablespoons lime juice
3 tablespoons light soy sauce
2 tablespoons fish sauce
2 tablespoons grated palm sugar or
  soft brown sugar
2 small red chillies, seeded and finely
  chopped

Heat a large, non-stick frying pan. Spray with the oil. Pat the meat dry with paper towels. Season well with black pepper. Put the meat in the pan and brown on both sides. Cook for a further 5–8 minutes, or until cooked as desired. Cover with foil and set aside for 5 minutes, then cut into thin slices.

Combine the dressing ingredients in a small bowl, stirring to dissolve the sugar.

Cover the noodles with boiling water and set aside for 5 minutes, or until softened. Drain and then cool. Use scissors to cut into smaller lengths.

Combine the cherry tomatoes, salad greens, cucumber, onion, radishes and the mint leaves in a large bowl. Toss through the noodles and the beef, then pour over the dressing. Serve immediately.

Serves 4

Warm mixed bean salad

2 tablespoons olive oil
125 ml (4 fl oz/½ cup) tomato juice
2 tablespoons chopped flat-leaf
  (Italian) parsley
pinch of sugar
3 garlic cloves
400 g (14 oz) tin borlotti beans,
  drained and rinsed
400 g (14 oz) tin cannellini beans,
  drained and rinsed
2 tomatoes, diced
4 thick slices crusty bread

Put 1 tablespoon of the oil in a small bowl with the tomato juice, parsley and sugar. Crush two of the garlic cloves and stir them into the mixture.

Put the borlotti and cannellini beans in a frying pan, add the tomato mixture and place over medium heat for about 5 minutes, or until well warmed through. Toss through the diced tomato and season to taste.

Meanwhile, toast bread slices. Cut the remaining garlic clove and rub the cut side all over bread. Drizzle with the remaining oil and then serve hot with the warm beans.

Serves 4

Warm pasta and crab salad

300 g (11 oz) thin spaghetti
2 tablespoons olive oil
20 g (1 oz) butter, chopped
350 g (12 oz) fresh crabmeat
1 red capsicum (pepper), cut into
  thin strips
1½ teaspoons finely grated lemon
  zest
3 tablespoons grated parmesan
  cheese
2 tablespoons snipped chives
3 tablespoons chopped parsley

Break all the spaghetti in half and cook in a large pot of rapidly boiling salted water until al dente. Drain well, then place in a large serving bowl and toss with the oil and butter.

Add crabmeat, capsicum, lemon zest, parmesan, chives and parsley, and toss to combine. Sprinkle with freshly ground black pepper and serve.

Serves 4

Warm salad of jerusalem artichoke, radicchio and pastrami

500 g (1 lb 2 oz) Jerusalem artichokes
juice of ½ lemon
pinch asafoetida
1 treviso radicchio
40 g (1½ oz/⅓ cup) golden walnut
  pieces
3 tablespoons walnut oil
1 small orange, zested and juiced
1 tablespoon shredded parsley
100 g (4 oz) pastrami slices, halved

Peel the artichokes. Cut any large ones to give pieces of roughly the same size. Put the artichokes in a non-reactive saucepan of boiling salted water with lemon juice and asafoetida. Simmer for 12 minutes, or until tender, then drain. When cool, slice the artichokes on the diagonal.

Preheat the grill (broiler) to hot. Trim off any coarse outer leaves from the radicchio and quarter it lengthways. Put the radicchio, cut side up, in a medium shallow heatproof dish, scatter the walnuts on top and then drizzle with half the oil. Grill (broil) for 1–2 minutes, or until leaves start to pucker and edges brown. Remove from the heat and set aside to cool for 2–3 minutes.

Cut off radicchio stems and return leaves to the dish. Add artichokes, orange juice and parsley and season with salt and freshly ground black pepper, to taste. Toss lightly. Scrunch the pastrami pieces into loose balls and arrange them among artichokes. Drizzle with remaining walnut oil and return to grill. Grill for 1–2 minutes, or until just beginning to brown. Top with orange zest and serve immediately.

Serves 4

Warm Thai tuna salad

650 g (1 lb 7 oz) fresh tuna steaks
1 tablespoon olive oil
2 tablespoons oyster sauce
2 tablespoons soy sauce
2 tablespoons lime juice
300 g (11 oz) dried egg noodles
125 g (5 oz) baby corn, halved
150 g (5 oz) snow peas (mangetout),
   tailed

Coriander chilli dressing
2 tablespoons fish sauce
2 tablespoons lime juice
2 tablespoons Thai sweet chilli sauce
2 tablespoons vegetable oil
1 small red chilli, chopped
3 tablespoons chopped coriander
   (cilantro)

Put tuna in a shallow dish in a single layer. Whisk together the oil, oyster sauce, soy sauce and lime juice and pour mixture over the tuna, turning to coat all over. Cover and refrigerate for 30 minutes.

Cook the noodles according to the packet instructions, adding corn and snow peas for the final 45 seconds. Drain well, then toss in a serving bowl. Combine dressing ingredients and mix half through the noodles.

Heat a chargrill pan (griddle) to high. Cook tuna for 3–4 minutes on each side, so it's still pink in middle. Cool slightly, then slice into strips. Serve separately or over the noodles, with remaining dressing on the side.

Serves 4

Warm prawn, rocket and feta salad

1 kg (2 lb 4 oz) raw prawns (shrimp)
4 spring onions (scallions), chopped
4 Roma (plum) tomatoes, chopped
1 red capsicum (pepper), chopped
400 g (14 oz) tinned chickpeas,
   drained and rinsed
1 tablespoon chopped dill
3 tablespoons finely shredded basil
1 tablespoon extra virgin olive oil
1 tablespoon reduced-fat olive or
   canola oil margarine
2 small red chillies, finely chopped
4 garlic cloves, crushed
2 tablespoons lemon juice
300 g (11 oz) rocket (arugula)
125 g (5 oz) low-fat feta cheese

Peel prawns, leaving the tails intact. Gently pull out dark vein from each prawn back, starting at the head end.

Combine the spring onion, tomato, capsicum, chickpeas and herbs in a bowl and mix well.

Heat the oil and margarine in a large frying pan or wok. Add the prawns and cook, stirring, over high heat for 3 minutes. Add chilli and garlic, and continue cooking until prawns turn pink. Remove from the heat and stir in the lemon juice.

Arrange the rocket leaves on a large platter, top with the tomato mixture, then the prawn mixture. Crumble the feta cheese over the top.

Serves 4–6

Pumpkin with chilli and avocado

750 g (1 lb 10 oz) winter squash
  pumpkin
1 large avocado

Dressing
1 small red onion
2 tablespoons olive oil
1 tablespoon chopped coriander
  (cilantro) leaves
1 tablespoon chopped mint
2 teaspoons sweet chilli sauce
2 teaspoons balsamic vinegar
1 teaspoon soft brown sugar

Scrape the seeds from the inside of the pumpkin. Cut the pumpkin into slices and remove the skin. Cook in a large saucepan of simmering water until tender but still firm. Remove from the heat and drain well.

To make the dressing, finely chop the red onion. Combine the onion with the remaining ingredients in a small bowl. Cut avocado in half. Remove stone using a sharp-bladed knife. Peel and discard skin from the avocado, then cut the flesh in thin slices.

Combine the warm pumpkin and the avocado in a serving bowl. Gently toss the coriander dressing through. Serve immediately.

Serves 6

Warm roasted potato with spicy sausage

800 g (1 lb 12 oz) small waxy
  potatoes, unpeeled
2 tablespoons olive oil
1 teaspoon sea salt
4 small chorizo sausages (about
  470 g/1 lb 1 oz), cut into
  1 cm (½ inch) slices
100 g (4 oz) rocket (arugula), leaves,
  trimmed and roughly torn
100 g (4 oz/²/₃ cup) semi-dried
  (sun-blushed) tomatoes
crusty bread, to serve

Seeded mustard dressing
3 tablespoons olive oil
1 tablepoon seeded mustard
2 tablespoons sherry vinegar or white
  wine vinegar

Preheat oven to 200°C (400°F/Gas 6).
Scrub the potatoes and then pat dry.
Put in a roasting tin without any oil or
seasoning and bake for 20 minutes,
or until starting to soften. Remove
from the oven and then gently squash
each potato using a potato masher,
until the skins burst and are slightly
flattened. Lightly drizzle oil over each
potato, sprinkle with the sea salt and
gently toss to coat. Roast for a further
about 10–15 minutes, or until crispy
and golden.

Meanwhile, put a frying pan over
high heat. Add chorizo and dry-fry
for about 5 minutes, or until cooked
through and golden. Transfer to a
serving dish along with rocket and
tomatoes.

Put all the seeded mustard dressing
ingredients in a small bowl. Whisk
well and season lightly with salt and
freshly ground black pepper.

Add the crispy potatoes to the salad,
pour the dressing over and toss well.
Serve hot or warm, with crusty bread.

Serves 4

Mini meatballs with couscous and yoghurt

600 g (1 lb 5 oz) lean minced (ground) beef
1 teaspoon chilli flakes
1 teaspoon ground cumin
2 tablespoons chopped pitted black olives
1 small onion, grated
2 tablespoons tomato paste (concentrated purée)
3–4 tablespoons olive oil
310 g (11 oz/3½ cups) instant couscous
250 g (9 oz) cherry tomatoes, halved
100 g (4 oz) roasted red capsicum (pepper), diced
200 g (7 oz) thick plain yoghurt
2 tablespoons lemon juice
2 tablespoons chopped parsley

Put beef, chilli flakes, cumin, olives, onion and tomato paste in a bowl. Season, mix well with your hands and roll into 40 balls. Chill for 30 minutes.

Put 275 ml (10 fl oz) water in a saucepan with 2 tablespoons of the oil and 2 teaspoons of salt. Bring to the boil, remove from heat and add the couscous. Stir, then cover and leave to stand for 2–3 minutes. Fluff up with a fork and add tomatoes and capsicum. Season and mix well.

Heat the remaining oil in a large frying pan. Fry meatballs over medium heat for 10–12 minutes, or until cooked through, then arrange them over the couscous. Mix yoghurt, lemon juice and parsley with 1 tablespoon water, drizzle over the meatballs and serve.

Serves 4

Warm salad of watercress, citrus and spring lamb

Dressing
1 tablespoon red wine vinegar
1 clove garlic, crushed
$1/2$ teaspoon honey
2 teaspoons walnut oil
$1\frac{1}{2}$ tablespoons olive oil

300 g (11 oz) lamb fillets
1 tablespoon olive oil
2 oranges
1 small pink grapefruit
3 large handfuls watercress,
  picked over
$1/2$ small red onion, finely sliced

To make the dressing, put all the ingredients in a small bowl, season with salt and freshly ground black pepper and whisk to combine.

Cut the lamb fillets in half and season with freshly ground black pepper. Heat olive oil in a frying pan over high heat and cook lamb for 3–4 minutes, or until browned, turning once or twice. Season with salt and remove from the heat.

Peel oranges and grapefruit, removing all the white pith. Holding them over a bowl to catch juice, segment them by using a sharp knife to cut between the membranes. Put segments in the bowl with the juices.

Cut the lamb on the diagonal into 2.5 cm (1 inch) thick slices and add to the bowl, along with watercress and red onion. Pour the dressing over the salad and lightly toss to coat.

Serves 4

Warm chicken, bean and pasta salad

750 g (1 lb 10 oz) orange sweet
   potato, peeled and cut into 2 cm
   (3/4 in) cubes
250 g (9 oz) cherry tomatoes, halved
olive oil spray
2 x 200 g (7 oz) boneless, skinless
   chicken breasts
350 g (12 oz/2 bunches) asparagus,
   trimmed and cut into thirds
375 g (13 oz) macaroni
400 g (14 oz) tin cannellini beans,
   drained and rinsed
3 handfuls baby rocket (arugula)
   leaves
3 tablespoons fat-free French
   dressing

Preheat oven to 200°C (400°F/Gas 6). Put the sweet potato in one end of a large non-stick roasting tin and the tomatoes in the other end, cut side down. Lightly spray with oil and then bake for 45 minutes, turning halfway through cooking time. Remove the tomatoes after 30 minutes.

Meanwhile, lightly spray a chargrill pan or barbecue chargrill plate with oil and heat to high. Cook the chicken for 5 minutes on each side, or until cooked through.

Bring a large saucepan of water to the boil. Add asparagus and cook for 1 minute, then remove with a slotted spoon and place into iced water. Drain. Return water to the boil and cook the macaroni for 10 minutes, or until tender. Drain and keep warm.

Slice chicken into 1 cm (1/2 inch) thick strips and place in a large bowl with roasted sweet potato and tomatoes, asparagus, pasta, the beans and the rocket and toss until combined. Add the dressing to salad and toss until well combined. Season with salt and freshly ground black pepper and then serve immediately.

Serves 6

Chargrilled vegetable salad with balsamic dressing

2 baby eggplants (aubergines)
2 large Roma (plum) tomatoes
1 red capsicum (pepper)
1/2 green capsicum (pepper)
1 zucchini (courgette)
2 1/2 tablespoons olive oil
6 bocconcini or 12 small, fresh
  mozzarella cheeses
12 Ligurian olives
1 garlic clove, finely chopped
1 heaped teaspoon baby capers,
  rinsed and drained
1/4 teaspoon sugar
1 tablespoon balsamic vinegar

Cut the eggplants and tomatoes into quarters. Cut the capsicums in half lengthways, remove the seeds and membrane, then cut each half into thick strips. Thinly slice the zucchini on the diagonal.

Preheat a chargrill pan (griddle) or barbecue hotplate to high. Brush with 1/2 tablespoon of the oil and cook the vegetables in batches for 2 minutes, or until slightly charred and golden, adding a little more oil as required. (The tomatoes are best cooked cut side down first.)

Put vegetables and cheese in a large bowl. Mix together the olives, garlic, capers, sugar and vinegar with the remaining oil, then pour over the salad and toss. Divide between two plates and serve.

Serves 2

Pesto beef salad

1 large red capsicum (pepper)
1 large yellow capsicum (pepper)
canola or olive oil spray
100 g (4 oz) lean beef fillet steak,
  trimmed
125 g (5 oz/1 1/3 cups) penne
100 g (4 oz) button mushrooms,
  quartered

Pesto
3 large handfuls basil
2 garlic cloves, chopped
2 tablespoons pepitas (pumpkin
  seeds)
1 tablespoon olive oil
2 tablespoons orange juice
1 tablepoon lemon juice

Cut capsicums into large flat pieces, removing the seeds and membrane. Put the skin side up under a hot grill (broiler) until blackened. Leave covered with a tea towel until cool, then peel away skin and chop flesh.

Spray a non-stick frying pan with oil and cook the steak over high heat for 3–4 minutes on each side. Remove and then leave for 5 minutes before cutting into thin slices. Season with a little salt.

To make pesto, finely chop the basil, garlic and pepitas in a food processor. With motor running, add oil, orange and lemon juice. Season well with salt and freshly ground black pepper.

Meanwhile, cook the pasta in a large saucepan of boiling water for about 10 minutes, or until al dente. Drain well and then toss along with pesto in a large bowl.

Add capsicum pieces, steak slices and mushroom quarters to the penne and toss to distribute evenly. Serve immediately.

Serves 4

Baked capsicums with anchovies

3 yellow capsicums (peppers)
3 red capsicums (peppers)
2 tablespoons extra virgin olive oil
12 anchovy fillets, halved lengthways
3 garlic cloves, thinly sliced
1 large handful basil, torn
1 tablespoon baby capers, rinsed
  and squeezed dry
extra virgin olive oil, to serve
sea salt, for sprinkling

Preheat the oven to 180°C (350°F/ Gas 4). Cut each capsicum in half lengthways, leaving stems intact. If capsicums are large, quarter them. Remove the seeds and membrane. Drizzle a little oil in a baking dish and place capsicums in, skin side down. Season well.

In each capsicum, place a halved anchovy fillet, some garlic and some of the basil. Divide the capers among the capsicums. Season and drizzle with the remaining oil.

Cover the dish with foil and bake the capsicums for 20 minutes. Remove foil and cook for 25–30 minutes, or until capsicums are tender. Drizzle them with a little extra virgin olive oil. Scatter the remaining basil over top, sprinkle with sea salt and serve warm or at room temperature.

Serves 6

Warm lamb salad

2 tablespoons red curry paste
3 tablespoons chopped coriander
  (cilantro) leaves
1 tablespoon finely grated ginger
1 tablespoon peanut oil
750 g (1 lb 10 oz) lamb loin fillets,
  trimmed and thinly sliced
200 g (7 oz) snow peas (mangetout),
  trimmed
600 g (1 lb 5 oz) thick fresh rice
  noodles
canola or olive oil spray
1 red capsicum (pepper), thinly sliced
1 Lebanese (short) cucumber, thinly
  sliced
6 spring onions (scallions), thinly
  sliced

Dressing
1 tablespoon peanut oil
3 tablespoons lime juice
2 teaspoons soft brown sugar
3 teaspoons fish sauce
3 teaspoons soy sauce
1 large hadful mint leaves, chopped
1 garlic clove, crushed

Combine the curry paste, coriander, ginger and oil in a bowl. Add the lamb and coat well. Cover and refrigerate for 2–3 hours.

Steam or boil the snow peas until just tender, then refresh under cold water and drain.

Put the noodles in a large heatproof bowl, cover with boiling water and soak for 8 minutes, or until softened. Separate gently and drain.

To make the dressing, put all the ingredients in a small bowl and whisk until well blended.

Heat a wok until very hot. Spray with the oil. Add half the lamb and stir-fry for 5 minutes, or until tender. Repeat with the remaining lamb, using more spray oil if needed.

Put the lamb, snow peas, noodles, capsicum, the cucumber and the spring onion in a large bowl, drizzle with the dressing and toss together before serving.

Serves 4-6

Warm pea, broad bean and potato salad

500 g (1 lb 2 oz) new or small waxy
    potatoes
2 tablespoons olive oil
1 onion, finely chopped
75 g (3 oz) smoked pancetta or
    bacon
2 cloves garlic, chopped
250 g (9 oz) podded, tender peas
200 g (7 oz) podded, tender broad
    (fava) beans
2 sprigs basil, torn
1 tablespoon red wine
1 tablespoon low-fat bio yoghurt,
    optional

Boil potatos until soft, drain and set aside. Heat oil in a large saucepan and add onion and pancetta. Cook over a medium heat for 5 minutes until onions are soft and the pancetta slightly caramelised. Add the garlic, reduce the heat and cook for a further minute.

Cut potatos in half lengthways or in large slices if they are big. Add the potatoes to the onions and then gently cook, stirring periodically for around 5 minutes more.

Blanch the peas for a few minutes in boiling water until cooked, then remove twith a slotted spoon and blanch the broad beans for a few minutes until soft. Drain and refresh broad beans in cold water. Remove the pale skin from any large broad beans and mix with peas. Add to the onions and stir breifly. Add basil and wine and cook for a further minute. Finally add the low-fat yoghurt if you are choosing to do so and remove from the heat. Serve on it's own as a light meal or to accompany grilled chicken breast or lamb chops.

Serves 4

Roast salmon with cucumber, ginger and chilli

6 x 200 g (7 oz) portions of skinned
  and boned salmon fillet
  (wild if possible)
3 tablespoons light soy sauce
3 tablespoons mirin (or sherry)
2 cucumbers
1 large chilli, halved and thinly sliced
1 teaspoon finely grated ginger
80 ml (3 fl oz/⅓ cup) rice vinegar or
  white wine vinegar
1 level tablespoon caster sugar
2 tablespoons fresh coriander
  (cilantro), coarsley chopped
1.3 kg (3 lb) new potatoes, cooked

Place the salmon in a flat-based dish, pour over the soy and mirin and turn to coat. Cover and allow to marinate for at least 30 minutes or overnight.

Peel cucumber, cut in half lengthways and then scoop out the seeds with a teaspoon. Thinly slice cucumber and place between sheets of kitchen towel to dry for about 5–10 minutes. Place cucumber in a bowl with the ginger, chilli, vinegar and sugar. Mix well and taste for seasoning. Leave to infuse all the flavours, though no longer than 3 hours or it will turn soggy.

Preheat oven to 200°C (400°F/Gas 6). Place salmon on a preheated roasting tray covered with foil. Drizzle over the marinade and cook salmon for about 10 minutes, until just cooked and still moist inside. Just before serving, add half of the chopped coriander to the cucumber mixture.

On each plate, either leave salmon fillets whole or divide into chunks, top with cucumber mixture and scatter over the remaining coriander leaves.

Serves 6

Warm goat's cheese salad with orange and hazelnut dressing

Hazelnut dressing
20 g (1 oz) hazelnuts
1 tablepoon orange juice
1 tablepoon lemon juice
125 ml (4 fl oz/½ cup) olive oil

2 oranges
250 g (9 oz) watercress, picked
50 g (2 oz) baby English spinach
  leaves
olive oil, for brushing
300 g (11 oz) goat's cheese, sliced
  into 4 portions

Preheat oven to 180°C (350°F/Gas 4). To make dressing, put hazelnuts on a baking tray and roast for 5–6 minutes, or until brown. Wrap the hazelnuts in a clean tea towel and rub together to remove the skins, then put them in a food processor with the orange juice, lemon juice and a pinch of salt. With the motor running, gradually add the oil a few drops at a time. When half the oil has been incorporated, add the remainder in a steady stream.

Peel rind and bitter white pith from the oranges. Cut the flesh into segments between the membrane, removing the seeds. Put segments in a large bowl along with watercress, spinach and 2 tablespoons of the dressing. Toss well and season to taste with pepper.

Heat a small, non-stick frying pan and brush lightly with olive oil. Press each slice of goat's cheese firmly into the pan and then cook over medium heat for 1–2 minutes, or until a crust forms underneath.

Arrange half the salad over four serving plates and put goat's cheese slices on top, crust side up. Scatter with the remaining salad, drizzle with the remaining dressing.

Serves 4

Warm minted chicken and pasta salad

250 g (9 oz) cotelli pasta
125 ml (4 fl oz/½ cup) olive oil
1 large red capsicum (pepper)
3 boneless, skinless chicken breasts
6 spring onions (scallions), cut into
 2 cm (¾ inch) lengths
4 garlic cloves, thinly sliced
3 large handfuls mint, chopped
80 ml (3 fl oz/⅓ cup) cider vinegar
100 g (4 oz) baby English
 spinach leaves

Cook the pasta in a large saucepan of boiling water until al dente, drain, stir in 1 tablespoon of the oil and set aside. Meanwhile, cut the capsicum into quarters, removing the seeds and membrane. Place, skin side up, under a hot grill (broiler) for 8–10 minutes, or until the skin blackens and blisters. Cool in a plastic bag, then peel away the skin. Cut into thin strips.

Place chicken between two sheets of plastic wrap and press with the palm of your hand until slightly flattened. Heat 1 tablespoon of the oil in a large frying pan, add the chicken and cook over medium heat for 2–3 minutes each side, or until light brown and cooked through. Remove from pan and cut into 5 mm (¼ inch) slices.

Add another tablespoon of oil to pan and add the spring onion, sliced garlic and capsicum and cook, stirring, for minutes, or until beginning to soften. Add two thirds of the mint, vinegar the remaining oil and stir until warmed through. In a large bowl, combine the pasta, the chicken, spinach, the onion mixture and remaining mint and toss well, seasoning to taste. Serve warm.

Serves 4

Warm pork salad with blue cheese croutons

125 ml (4 fl oz/½ cup) olive oil
1 large garlic clove, crushed
400 g (14 oz) pork fillet, cut into
   5 mm (¼ inch) slices
1 small or ½ a large baguette, cut
   into 20 x 5 mm (¼ inch) slices
100 g (4 oz) blue cheese, crumbled
2 tablespoons sherry vinegar
½ teaspoon soft brown sugar
150 g (5 oz) mixed salad leaves

Place the olive oil and garlic in a jar and shake well. Heat 2 teaspoons of the garlic oil in a frying pan, add half the pork and cook for 1 minute on each side. Remove and keep warm. Add another 2 teaspoons garlic oil and then cook the remaining pork. Remove. Season pork with salt and pepper to taste.

Lay the bread slices on a baking tray and brush with a little garlic oil on one side. Cook the bread under a hot griller (broiler) until golden. Turn the bread over, sprinkle with the crumbled blue cheese, then return to the griller and cook until the cheese has melted (this will happen very quickly).

Add the sherry vinegar and sugar to the remaining garlic oil and shake well. Place the salad leaves in a large bowl, add the pork and pour on the salad dressing. Toss well. Place a mound of salad in the middle of four serving plates and then arrange five croutons around the edge of each salad. Serve the salad immediately.

Serves 4

Marinated prawns with corn and chickpea salsa

400 g (14 oz) tin cannellini beans,
   drained and rinsed
300 g (11 oz) tin chickpeas, drained
   and rinsed
310 g (11 oz) tin corn kernels, drained
   and rinsed
1 teaspoon grated lime zest
2 tablespoons chopped coriander
   (cilantro) leaves
500 g (1 lb 2 oz) large raw prawns
   (shrimp)
2 tablespoons lemon juice
1 tablespoon sesame oil
2 garlic cloves, crushed
2 teaspoons grated ginger
canola or olive oil spray
lime wedges, to serve

Combine cannellini beans, chickpeas and corn kernels in a large bowl. Stir in the lime zest and coriander.

Peel the prawns, leaving the tails intact. Gently pull out the dark vein from each prawn back, starting at the head end.

To make the marinade, combine the lemon juice, the sesame oil, the garlic and the ginger in a small bowl. Add the prawns and gently stir to coat in marinade. Cover and refrigerate for at least 3 hours.

Lightly spray a barbecue hotplate with oil and heat to high. Add prawns and cook for 3–5 minutes, or until pink and cooked through. Brush frequently with marinade while cooking. Serve immediately with the corn, bean and chickpea salsa and wedges of lime.

Serves 4

Tuscan warm pasta salad

500 g (1 lb 2 oz) rigatoni
80 ml (3 fl oz/⅓ cup) olive oil
1 garlic clove, crushed
1 tablespoon balsamic vinegar
425 g (15 oz) tinned artichoke hearts,
    drained and quartered
8 thin prosciutto slices, chopped
80 g (3 oz/½ cup) sun-dried tomatoes
    in oil, drained and thinly sliced
2 handfuls basil, shredded
70 g (3 oz) rocket (arugula), washed
    and well drained
3 tablespoons pine nuts, toasted
3 tablespoons black Italian olives

Add the rigatoni to a large saucepan
of rapidly boiling water and cook until
al dente. Drain the pasta thoroughly
and transfer to a large bowl.

While the pasta is cooking, whisk
together the oil, garlic and balsamic
vinegar. Toss dressing through the hot
pasta. Allow the pasta to cool slightly.
Add the artichoke hearts, prosciutto,
sun-dried tomato, basil, rocket, pine
nuts and olives.

Toss all the ingredients together until
well combined. Season to taste.

Serves 6

Baked radicchio

1 kg (2 lb 4 oz) radicchio
2 tablespoons olive oil
100 g (4 oz) bacon, thinly sliced

Preheat oven to 180°C (350°F/Gas 4). Remove outer leaves of the radicchio and split the heads into four wedges.

Heat the olive oil in a flameproof casserole dish large enough to fit all the radicchio in a single layer (but do not add radicchio yet). Add the bacon and cook over medium heat until the fat has just melted but the meat is not crisp. Add radicchio and then turn it over to coat it well. Bake, covered, for 25–30 minutes, until tender when pierced with a knife, turning radicchio occasionally. Season and transfer to a warm dish with all the liquid. Serve immediately.

Serves 4

Spinach with raisins and pine nuts

500 g (1 lb 2 oz) English spinach
1 small red onion
2 tablespoons pine nuts
1 tablespoon olive oil
1 garlic clove, thinly sliced
2 tablespoons raisins
pinch of ground cinnamon

Trim the stalks from the spinach and discard. Wash and shred the leaves. Slice the onion.

Put the pine nuts in a frying pan and stir over medium heat for 3 minutes, or until lightly brown. Remove from the pan.

Heat the oil in the pan, add onion and cook over low heat, stirring every now and then, for 10 minutes, or until it is translucent. Increase heat to medium, add garlic and cook for 1 minute. Add spinach with the water clinging to it, the raisins and cinnamon. Cover and cook for 2 minutes, or until spinach wilts. Stir in pine nuts, and season with salt and pepper to taste.

Serves 4

Cooked vegetable salad

1 small turnip
1 large onion
2 celery stalks
200 g (7 oz) button mushrooms
1 large carrot
1/2 red capsicum (pepper)
4 spring onions (scallions)
2 tablespoons sesame oil
1 tablespoon vegetable oil
2 garlic cloves, finely chopped
80 g (3 oz/1/2 cup) pine nuts, toasted
  (see Note)

Dressing
3 tablespoons soy sauce
1 tablespoon white vinegar
3 cm (1 1/4 inch) piece ginger, very
  finely sliced and cut into fine strips
1–2 teaspoons soft brown sugar

Cut turnip into thin strips. Slice the onion, celery stalks and the button mushrooms. Cut the carrot into fine strips. Cut the red capsicum in half, remove seeds and membrane and cut into fine strips. Chop spring onions.

Put turnip on a plate lined with paper towel. Sprinkle with 2 teaspoons of salt and then set aside for at least 20 minutes. Rinse turnip under cold water and pat dry with paper towel.

Heat combined oils in a large frying pan or wok and swirl to coat the base and side. Stir-fry the turnip, garlic and the onion for 3 minutes over medium heat, or until lightly golden. Add red capsicum, celery, mushrooms, carrot and spring onion and toss well. Cover and steam for 1 minute. Remove the the vegetables from the wok and set aside to cool.

To make dressing, combine all the ingredients in a bowl. Pour dressing over the cooled vegetables and toss. Arrange them on a serving plate and sprinkle with the pine nuts.

Serves 4

Note: Toast the pine nuts in a dry frying pan over medium heat, stirring constantly, until they are golden brown and fragrant.

Grilled vegetables with garlic mayonnaise

2 eggplants (aubergines), cut
  into thin slices
4 small leeks, white part only
4 small zucchini (courgettes)
2 red capsicums (peppers)
8 large flat mushrooms

Dressing
1 tablespoon balsamic vinegar
2 tablespoons Dijon mustard
2 teaspoons dried oregano leaves
250 ml (9 fl oz/1 cup) olive oil

Garlic mayonnaise
2 egg yolks
1 tablespoon lemon juice
2 garlic cloves, crushed
250 ml (9 fl oz/1 cup) olive oil
1 tablespoon snipped chives
1 tablespoon chopped flat-leaf
  (Italian) parsley

Sprinkle eggplant with salt and leave to stand for 30 minutes. Rinse under cold water, then pat dry with paper towel. Halve the leeks and zucchinis lengthways. Cut the capsicum in half, remove the seeds and membrane and cut each half into four pieces.

To make dressing, combine vinegar, mustard and oregano in a bowl, then gradually whisk in the oil. Preheat the grill (broiler) to high. Place eggplant, leek, zucchini and capsicum in a single layer on a flat grill tray, then brush with some dressing. Cook under the grill on high for 5 minutes. Turn the vegetables once, brushing occasionally with dressing. Add the mushrooms to the grill tray and brush them with dressing. Continue cooking the vegetables for 10 minutes, or until tender, turning the mushrooms once.

To make the mayonnaise, put the egg yolks, lemon juice and garlic in a food processor or blender and blend for 5 seconds until combined. With the motor running, add oil slowly in a thin, steady stream until it is all added and mayonnaise is thick and creamy. Add the chives, parsley and 1 tablespoon water and blend until well combined. Serve with grilled vegetables.

Serves 8

A World
of Flavours

Thai-style chicken salad

4 skinless, boneless chickens breasts,
  cut into 1 cm (½ inch) strips
1 teaspoon grated fresh ginger
1 garlic clove, crushed
2 tablespoons soy sauce
1 tablespoon peanut oil
3 spring onions (scallions), sliced
  diagonally
2 carrots, julienned
35 g (1 oz) snow pea (mangetout)
  sprouts

Dressing
2 tablespoons sweet chilli sauce
1 tablespoon rice vinegar
2 tablespoons peanut oil

Put the chicken in a non-metallic dish.
Mix together the ginger, garlic and soy
sauce and smother mixture all over
the chicken. Cover and refrigerate for
at least 2 hours, or overnight, turning
every now and then.

Nearer to serving time, put all the
dressing ingredients in a small
screw-top jar and shake well.

Heat oil in a heavy-based pan. Add
the chicken and cook in batches over
medium heat for 3–4 minutes, or until
cooked and nicely browned.

Drain on crumpled paper towels and
then set aside to cool, then place in a
serving bowl with spring onion, carrot
and snow pea sprouts. Pour dressing
over top and toss lightly to combine.
Serve immediately.

Serves 4

Tunisian eggplant salad with preserved lemon

2 large eggplants (aubergines)
125 ml (4 fl oz/½ cup) olive oil
1 teaspoon cumin seeds
2 cloves garlic, very thinly sliced
1 tablespoon currants
1 tablespoon slivered almonds
6 small Roma (plum) tomatoes, quartered lengthways
1 teaspoon dried oregano
4 red bird's eye chillies, halved lengthways and seeded
2 tablespoons lemon juice
1 large handful flat-leaf (Italian) parsley, chopped
½ preserved or salted lemon
extra virgin olive oil to serve

Cut the eggplants into 2 cm (¾ inch) cubes, put in a large colander and sprinkle with 1–2 teaspoons salt. Set aside to drain in the sink for about 2–3 hours. Dry with paper towels.

Heat half of the olive oil in a large flameproof casserole dish over medium heat. Fry the eggplant in batches for 5–6 minutes, or until golden, adding more oil as needed.

Drain on crumpled paper towels. Reduce heat and add any remaining oil to casserole dish, along with the cumin, garlic, currants and almonds. Fry for 20–30 seconds, or until garlic starts to colour. Add the tomato and oregano and then cook for 1 minute.

Remove from heat. Trim rind from the piece of preserved lemon and cut the rind into thin strips. Discard the flesh.

Return eggplant to casserole and add the chilli, the lemon juice, parsley and preserved lemon rind. Toss gently and season with ground black pepper. Set aside at room temperature for 1 hour before serving. Check the seasoning, then drizzle with extra olive oil.

Serves 4

Asian-style coleslaw

200 g (7 oz/2²/₃ cups) finely shredded
   red cabbage
175 g (6 oz/4 cups) finely shredded
   Chinese cabbage
1 large carrot
1 small red onion
1 red chilli, seeded, optional
80 g (3 oz/³/₄ cup) thinly sliced snow
   peas (mangetout)
1 small handful Thai (holy) basil, torn
50 g (2 oz/¹/₃ cup roasted peanuts,
   coarsely chopped

Dressing
2 tablespooons lime juice
1¹/₂ tablespoons finely grated ginger
90 g (3 oz/¹/₃ cup) light sour cream
1 teaspoon fish sauce
1 garlic clove, crushed

Combine red cabbage and Chinese
cabbage in a large bowl. Peel carrot
and shave it with a vegetable peeler.
Thinly slice onion and the chilli. Add
the carrot, onion and chilli to the bowl
along with the snow peas, basil and
2 tablespoons of peanuts. Toss to
combine well.

To make dressing, put all ingredients
in a small bowl and whisk until they
are combined. Pour over the cabbage
mixture and toss well to coat. Scatter
remaining peanuts on top. Serve at
room temperature.

Serves 4

Russian salad

Mayonnaise
2 eggs, separated
1 teaspoon Dijon mustard
125 ml (4 fl oz/½ cup) extra virgin
   olive oil
2 tablespoons lemon juice
2 small cloves garlic, crushed

3 canned artichoke hearts
3 waxy potatoes, such as desiree,
   unpeeled
100 g (3½ oz) baby green beans,
   trimmed and cut into 1 cm (½ inch)
   lengths
1 large carrot, cut into 1 cm (½ inch)
   dice
125 g (4½ oz) fresh or frozen peas
30 g (1 oz) cornichons, chopped
2 tablespoons baby capers, rinsed
4 anchovy fillets, finely chopped
10 black olives, each cut into 3 slices,
   plus 5 extra to garnish

To make mayonnaise, use electric beaters to beat egg yolks with Dijon mustard and ¼ teaspoon salt until creamy. Gradually add oil in a slow, fine stream, beating constantly until all oil has been added. Add lemon juice, garlic and 1 teaspoon boiling water and beat for 1 minute, or until well combined. Season to taste.

Cut each artichoke into quarters. Rinse potatoes, put in a saucepan, cover with cold salted water and bring to a gentle simmer. Cook for 15–20 minutes, or until tender when pierced with a knife. Drain well and then allow to cool slightly. Peel and set aside. When potatoes are cool, cut into 1 cm (½ inch) dice.

Blanch beans in boiling salted water until tender but still firm to the bite. Refresh in cold water, then drain well. Repeat with the carrot and the peas.

Set aside a small quantity of each vegetable, including the chopped cornichons, for the garnish and then season to taste. Put remainder in a bowl with the capers, anchovies and sliced olives. Add mayonnaise, toss to combine and season. Arrange on a serving dish and garnish with the reserved vegetables and whole olives.

Serves 4 to 6

Tandoori lamb salad

250 g (9 oz/1 cup) low-fat natural
  yoghurt
2 cloves garlic, crushed
2 teaspoons grated ginger
2 teaspoons ground turmeric
2 teaspoons garam masala
1/4 teaspoon paprika
2 teaspoons ground coriander
red food colouring, optional
500 g (1 lb 2 oz) lean lamb fillets
80 ml (3 fl oz/1/3 cup) lemon juice
1 1/2 teaspoons chopped coriander
  (cilantro)
1 teaspoon chopped fresh mint
150 g (5 oz) mixed salad leaves
1 large mango, cut into strips
2 cucumbers, cut into matchsticks

Mix the yoghurt, the garlic, ginger and
spices in a bowl, add a little colouring
and toss with the lamb to coat well.
Cover and then refrigerate overnight.

Grill lamb on a foil-lined baking tray
under high heat for 7 minutes each
side, or until the marinade starts to
brown. Set aside for 5 minutes
before serving.

Mix the lemon juice, the coriander and
mint, then season. Toss with the salad
leaves, the mango and the cucumber,
then arrange on plates. Slice the lamb
and serve over the salad.

Serves 4

Seared Asian salmon salad

700 g (1 lb 9 oz) salmon fillets
1 tablespoon olive oil
2 tablespoons lime juice
1 tablespoon soy sauce
2 tablespoons runny honey
2 ripe mangoes, thinly sliced
200 g (7 oz) bean sprouts,
    tails trimmed
1 small cos (romaine) lettuce, leaves
    separated
1 handful coriander (cilantro) leaves

Asian dressing
1 tablespoon olive oil
1 tablespoon fish sauce
2 tablespoons lime juice
1 small red chilli, finely chopped
½ teaspoon sugar

Remove any pin bones from salmon and put the fillets in a single layer in a shallow non-metallic dish. In a small bowl, whisk oil, lime juice, soy sauce and honey. Pour mixture over salmon, ensuring it coats all sides of the fish. Cover and refrigerate for 30 minutes. Meanwhile, put dressing ingredients in a small bowl and whisk until well combined. Set aside until needed.

Preheat a barbecue grill or chargrill pan (griddle) to high. If you like your salmon slightly pink in middle, cook fillets for 5 minutes on one side, then turn and cook the second side for a further 4 minutes. If you prefer it cooked all the way through, leave it for an extra minute on second side. Cooking times will vary depending on heat of your barbecue and thickness of salmon fillets. Leave the salmon to cool slightly, then break into chunks.

Put mango, bean sprouts and lettuce leaves in a serving bowl, add salmon chunks and toss gently. Pour over the dressing, scatter with coriander and serve at once.

Serves 4

Note: Add dressing just before serving so the salad doesn't become soggy.

Pacific chicken salad

250 ml (9 fl oz/1 cup) coconut milk
1 tablespoon fish sauce
1 tablespoon grated palm sugar
4 skinless, boneless chicken breasts
2 mangoes, thinly sliced
4 spring onions (scallions), sliced
1 handful coriander (cilantro) leaves
45 g (1½ oz/⅓ cup) coarsely
  chopped roasted unsalted
  macadamia nuts

Dressing
2 tablespoons oil
1 teaspoon finely grated lime zest
2 tablespoons lime juice

Place coconut milk, fish sauce and palm sugar in a frying pan and bring to the boil, stirring. Reduce heat, add the chicken fillets and simmer gently, covered, for 10 minutes, or until the chicken is just tender. Leave to cool in the coconut liquid, then remove and pour the liquid into a jug.

To make the dressing, put 125 ml (4 fl oz/½ cup) of reserved coconut cooking liquid, the oil, lime zest and juice in a small bowl and whisk to combine. Season to taste with salt and pepper.

Cut each chicken fillet diagonally into long slices and then arrange them on individual serving plates or in a large serving bowl. Spoon dressing over the chicken and top with macadamia nuts, the sliced mango, spring onion and the coriander leaves

Serves 4

Note: Palm sugar is obtained from either the palmyra palm or the sugar palm, and is available in block form or in jars. It can be grated or gently melted before using. Soft brown is a good substitute.

Thai noodle salad

250 g (9 oz) dried instant egg noodles
500 g (1 lb 2 oz) cooked large prawns
(shrimp), peeled and deveined,
tails intact
5 spring onions (scallions), sliced
2 tablespoons chopped coriander
(cilantro)
1 red capsicum (pepper), diced
100 g (4 oz) snow peas (mangetout),
julienned
4 lime wedges

Dressing
2 tablespoons grated ginger
2 tablespoons soy sauce
2 tablespoons sesame oil
80 ml (3 fl oz/⅓ cup) red wine vinegar
1 tablespoons sweet chilli sauce
2 garlic cloves, crushed
80 ml (3 fl oz/⅓ cup) kecap manis

Cook the egg noodles in a pot of boiling water for 2 minutes, or until tender. Drain thoroughly, then leave to cool in a large serving bowl.

Whisk all the dressing ingredients together in a bowl and gently mix through the cooled noodles. Add the prawns, the spring onion, the coriander, capsicum and the snow peas. Toss gently and serve with lime wedges.

Serves 4

Greek peppered lamb salad

300 g (11 oz) lamb backstraps
  or fillets
1½ tablespoons black pepper
3 vine-ripened tomatoes, cut into
  8 wedges
2 Lebanese (short) cucumbers, sliced
150 g (5 oz) lemon and garlic
  marinated Kalamata olives, drained
  (reserving 1½ tablespoons oil)
100 g (4 oz) Greek feta cheese,
  cubed
¾ teaspoon dried oregano
1 tablespoon lemon juice
1 tablespoon extra virgin olive oil

Roll the backstraps in the pepper, pressing the pepper on with your fingers. Cover and refrigerate for 15 minutes.

Place tomato, cucumber, olives, feta and ½ teaspoon of the dried oregano in a bowl.

Heat a chargrill pan or a barbecue hotplate, brush with oil and when very hot, cook the lamb for 2–3 minutes on each side, or until cooked to your liking. Keep warm.

Whisk together the lemon juice, extra virgin olive oil, reserved Kalamata oil and remaining dried oregano. Season. Pour half the dressing over the salad, toss together and then arrange on a serving platter.

Cut the lamb on diagonal into 1 cm (½ inch) thick slices and arrange on top of salad. Pour remaining dressing on top and serve.

Serves 4

Poached chicken and greens with sesame miso dressing

4 skinless, boneless, chicken breasts
3 black peppercorns
3 slices ginger
3 spring onions (scallions), sliced
200 g (7 oz) mangetout (snow peas)
200 g (7 oz) asparagus, cut into 4 cm
  (1½ inch) lengths
100 g (4 oz) green beans, cut into
  4 cm (1½ inch) lengths

Sesame miso dressing
1 teaspoon sesame oil
2 teaspoons white miso
3 tablespoons mirin or sherry
3 tablespoons low-salt soy sauce
2 tablespoons seasoned rice vinegar
2 tablespoons black sesame seeds
700 g (1 lb 9 oz) pilau rice (cooked
  weight), to serve

Trim the chicken breast fillets of any excess fat and sinew. Half-fill a large deep frying pan with water, add the peppercorns, the ginger and spring onions and chicken. Simmer them gently for 20 minutes or until chicken is tender. Remove the chicken and allow it to cool slightly.

Steam the mangetout, asparagus and beans until tender then arrange them on a platter. Shred the chicken in thin strips and arrange these on top of the vegetables. Put dressing ingredients into a small pan and whisk over a medium heat until the miso dissolves.

Drizzle dressing over the salad and sprinkle on the black sesame seeds.

Serves 4

Mediterranean lentil salad

1 large red capsicum (pepper)
1 large yellow capsicum (pepper)
250 g (9 oz/1 cup) red lentils
1 red onion, finely chopped
1 Lebanese (short) cucumber,
    chopped

Dressing
80 ml (3 fl oz/⅓ cup) olive oil
2 tablespoons lemon juice
1 teaspoon ground cumin
2 garlic cloves, crushed

Cut capsicums in half lengthways. Remove the seeds and membrane and then cut capsicums into large, flattish pieces. Grill (broil) them until the skin blackens and blisters. Put capsicum on a cutting board, cover with a tea towel (dish towel) and then leave to cool. Peel capsicum and cut the flesh into 5 mm (¼ inch) strips.

Cook the lentils in boiling water for 10 minutes, or until tender (take care not to overcook, or they will become mushy). Drain well. Put the capsicum, lentils, onion and cucumber in a bowl and toss to combine.

To make dressing, put olive oil, lemon juice, cumin, garlic and some salt and pepper into a small bowl and whisk to combine. Pour the dressing over the salad and mix well. Cover salad and then refrigerate for 4 hours. Allow the salad to return to room temperature before serving.

Serves 4–6

Vietnamese cucumber salad with steamed fish

Salad

1 teaspoon lime juice
2 tablespoons sweet chilli sauce
1–2 tablespoons fish sauce
1/2–1 tablespoon grated palm sugar
  (or raw caster (superfine) sugar)
4 Lebanese (short) cucumbers, cut
  into 2 cm (3/4 inch) chunks
1/2 red onion, sliced
1 large pear
1 small handful Vietnamese mint
1 small handful Thai basil

2 stems lemongrass, trimmed, finely
  chopped
80 ml (3 fl oz/1/3 cup) fish sauce
3 tablespoons palm sugar, or raw
  caster (superfine) sugar
1 kg (2 lb 4 oz) cod fillets
80 g (3 oz/1/2 cup) roasted unsalted
  peanuts, chopped

To make salad, combine the lime juice and sweet chilli sauce in a large bowl and add fish sauce and palm sugar, to taste. Add the cucumber and the onion. Quarter and core pear, slice it thinly and add it to the bowl. Chop half the mint and basil leaves, add to the bowl and toss to coat. Cover and set aside in a cool place for 2 hours.

Meanwhile, combine the lemongrass, fish sauce and palm sugar in a large bowl. Slice the cod into 1 cm (1/2 inch) thick slices and add to the bowl. Toss to coat, cover with plastic wrap and chill for 1 hour.

Line a large bamboo steamer with baking paper and cover with as many slices of cod as will fit in a single layer. Place over a wok or a saucepan of boiling water. Steam for 4 minutes, or until cooked through. Repeat with the rest of the fish.

To serve, toss the remaining mint leaves and the peanuts through the salad. Divide among four serving plates and top with the fish and the remaining basil leaves.

Serves 4

Tuscan bread salad

200 g (7 oz) ciabatta bread
8 vine-ripened tomatoes
80 ml (3 fl oz/⅓ cup) olive oil
1 tablespoon lemon juice
1½ tablespoons red wine vinegar
6 anchovy fillets, finely chopped
1 tablespoon baby capers, rinsed,
    drained and finely chopped
1 garlic clove, crushed
30 g (1 oz/1 cup) basil leaves

Preheat the oven to 220°C (425°F/ Gas 7). Tear bread into 2 cm (¾ inch) pieces, spread on a baking tray and bake for 5–7 minutes, or until golden on outside. Leave the toasted bread on a cake rack to cool.

Score a cross in the base of each tomato. Place in a heatproof bowl and cover with boiling water. Leave for 30 seconds, then transfer to cold water and peel the skin away from the cross. Cut four of the tomatoes in half and squeeze juice and seeds into a bowl, reserving and chopping the flesh. Add the oil, juice, vinegar, anchovies, capers and the garlic to the tomato juice, and season.

Seed and slice remaining tomatoes, and place in a large bowl along with the reserved tomato and most of the basil. Add the dressing and toasted bread, and toss. Garnish with the remaining basil, season, and then leave for at least 15 minutes. Serve at room temperature.

Serves 6

Chilli squid with Asian salad

8 squid
270 g (10 oz) packet dried udon
  noodles
1 small red capsicum (pepper)
3 Asian shallots
200 g (7 oz) baby Asian salad leaves
180 g (6 oz/2 cups) bean sprouts
oil spray

Marinade
zest and juice from 1 lemon
2 tablespoon sweet chilli sauce
1 tablespoon grated palm sugar or
  soft brown sugar
1 teaspoon canola oil

Lemon dressing
3 tablespoons lemon juice
3 tablespoons rice wine vinegar
2 tablespoons grated palm sugar or
  soft brown sugar
1½ tablespoons fish sauce
1 small red chilli, seeded and
  chopped

To clean squid, remove head, insides and the beak. Wash squid well under cold water and pull away outer skin. Cut off tentacles from heads. Score skin in a zigzag pattern and cut into 5 cm (2 inch) pieces. Combine the marinade, the squid pieces and the tentacles in a large, non-metallic bowl and then refrigerate for 30 minutes, or longer if possible.

Meanwhile, cook the noodles in a large saucepan of boiling water for 10 minutes, or follow manufacturer's directions. Drain, rinse well in cold water and drain again. Cut noodles into shorter lengths with scissors.

Seed and thinly slice capsicum. Thinly slice shallots on diagonal. Place the salad leaves, the capsicum, shallots, the bean sprouts and the noodles in a serving bowl.

Combine the dressing ingredients in a bowl. Drain squid. Heat a barbecue flat plate or frying pan and then lightly spray with oil. Cook and toss squid over a high heat for 2 minutes, or until cooked. Add squid to salad and toss together with the lemon dressing. Serve immediately.

Serves 4

Fennel, orange and almond salad

2 fennel bulbs, trimmed
3 oranges
100 g (4 oz) flaked almonds
150 g (5 oz) creamy blue cheese, crumbled
50 g (2 oz) sun-dried (sun-blushed) capsicum (pepper), thinly sliced (see Note)

Dressing
80 ml (3 fl oz/⅓ cup) orange juice
1 tablespoon red wine vinegar
1 teaspoon sesame oil

Thinly slice the fennel bulbs. Peel the oranges, removing all the white pith, and cut into segments. Toast the flaked almonds in a dry frying pan until golden.

Combine fennel, orange and almonds in a bowl. Add crumbled blue cheese and sun-dried capsicum. Gently toss to combine.

Make dressing by combining orange juice, red wine vinegar and sesame oil. Drizzle over the salad and serve.

Serves 4

Note: Pat sun-dried capsicum with paper towels to remove excess oil.

Indian marinated chicken salad

3 tablespoons lemon juice
1½ teaspoons garam masala
1 teaspoon ground turmeric
1 tablespoon finely grated ginger
2 garlic cloves, finely chopped
3½ tablespoons oil
3 skinless, boneless chicken breast
  fillets (650 g/1 lb 7 oz)
1 onion, thinly sliced
2 zucchini (courgettes), thinly sliced
  on the diagonal
100 g (4 oz/3½ cups) watercress
  leaves
150 g (5½ oz/1 cup) freshly shelled
  peas
2 ripe tomatoes, finely chopped
3 handuls coriander (cilantro) leaves

Dressing
1 teaspoon cumin seeds
½ teaspoon coriander seeds
90 g (3 oz/⅓ cup) natural yoghurt
2 tablespoons chopped mint
2 tablespoons lemon juice

Combine the lemon juice, the garam masala, turmeric, the ginger, the garlic and 2 teaspoons of oil in a large bowl. Add the chicken fillets and the onion, toss to coat in marinade, cover and refrigerate for 1 hour.

Remove and discard onion, then heat 2 tablespoons of oil in a large frying pan. Cook chicken for 4–5 minutes on each side, or until cooked through. Remove chicken from pan and leave for 5 minutes. Cut each breast across the grain into 1 cm (½ inch) slices.

Heat the remaining oil in the pan and cook the zucchini for 2 minutes, or until lightly golden and tender. Toss `with watercress in a large bowl. Cook peas in boiling water for 5 minutes, or until tender, then drain. Rinse under cold water to cool. Add to salad with the tomato, chicken and coriander.

For dressing, gently roast the cumin and coriander seeds in a dry frying pan for 1–2 minutes, or until fragrant. Remove, then pound the seeds to a powder. Mix with yoghurt, mint and lemon juice, then gently fold through the salad.

Serves 4

Daikon with sashimi

Dipping sauce
125 ml (4 fl oz/½ cup) Japanese soy
  sauce
1 teaspoon grated ginger
a pinch of sugar

Daikon salad
150 g (5 oz) daikon, peeled
1 Lebanese (short) cucumber
1 carrot, peeled
4 cm (1½ inch) ginger piece
3 spring onions (scallions), thinly
  sliced on the diagonal
½ teaspoon sesame seeds, roasted
2 teaspoons rice vinegar
2 teaspoons Japanese soy sauce
2 teaspoons mirin
1 sheet nori, roasted
250 g (9 oz) piece sashimi-quality
  salmon
250 g (9 oz) piece sashimi-quality
  tuna
wasabi paste, to serve

To make dipping sauce, stir the soy sauce, ginger and sugar in a small bowl until the sugar has dissolved. Divide the sauce among four small dishes and then place them on four serving plates.

To make the salad, shave the daikon, cucumber and the carrot lengthways into wide thin strips with a mandolin or a vegetable peeler and put in a large bowl. Cut the ginger into fine matchsticks and add to the bowl.

Just before you are ready to serve, add the spring onion, sesame seeds, rice vinegar, soy sauce and mirin and toss to coat. Divide the salad among the serving plates.

Cut nori into thin strips using scissors and scatter some over each salad. Using a very sharp knife, slice salmon and the tuna into even 5 mm (¼ inch) thick strips. Divide among the plates, arranging them in neat rows. Add a dab of wasabi to the plates and serve.

Serves 4

Moroccan lamb salad

Spice mix
2 garlic cloves, crushed
1 teaspoon ground cumin
1 teaspoon harissa
1 teaspoon ground coriander

125 ml (4 fl oz/½ cup) olive oil
2 large handfuls coriander, finely
  chopped
2 tablespoons lemon juice
3 tablespoons chopped parsley
½ teaspoon ground turmeric
2 lamb backstraps or loin fillets
  (600 g/1 lb 5 oz), trimmed
250 g (9 oz/1 cup) thick plain yoghurt
50 g (2 oz) baby rocket (arugula)

Pistachio couscous
125 ml (4 fl oz/½ cup) orange juice
2 tablespoons lemon juice
½ teaspoon ground cinnamon
250 g (9 oz/1⅓ cups) instant
  couscous
50 g (2 oz) butter
3 tablespoons currants
50 g (2 oz/heaped ⅓ cup) chopped
  pistachio nuts
425 g (15 oz) tin chickpeas, rinsed
  and drained
3 tablespoons chopped parsley

In a small bowl, combine the spice mix ingredients. Put the oil in a large, non-metallic bowl and stir in half the spice mix and all the coriander, lemon juice, parsley and turmeric. Mix well. Add lamb, turning to coat well. Cover with plastic wrap and refrigerate for 1 hour. Mix the remaining spice mix with the yoghurt, cover and refrigerate until needed.

To make pistachio couscous, pour the orange and the lemon juice into a measuring jug, then add enough water to make 300 ml (10½ fl oz). Pour into a saucepan, add cinnamon and bring to the boil. Remove from heat, pour in couscous, cover and leave for 5 minutes. Add butter and fluff up couscous with a fork, raking out any lumps, then fold in currants, pistachios, chickpeas and parsley.

Meanwhile, preheat a barbecue grill or chargrill pan (griddle) to high. Drain marinade from lamb and then cook for 2 minutes on each side, or until charred on outside but pink in middle. Remove from heat, cover with foil and rest for 5 minutes, then slice across the grain. Divide couscous between four large serving plates and top with the rocket and lamb slices. Top with a dollop of yoghurt mixture and serve.

Serves 4

Asian chicken salad with black vinegar dressing

600 g (1 lb 5 oz) skinless, boneless
  chicken breasts
1 large carrot, julienned
100 g (4 oz) baby Asian greens
1 Lebanese (short) cucumber,
  julienned
200 g (7 oz/2 heaped cups) bean
  sprouts, tails trimmed
3 spring onions (scallions), sliced
  on the diagonal
1 small handful Thai basil leaves

Black vinegar dressing
2 tablespoons black vinegar
2 tablespoons kecap manis
1½ tablespoons soy sauce
1 teaspoon sesame oil
2 tablespoons vegetable oil
5 cm (2 inch) piece of ginger, peeled
  and grated

Heat a barbecue hotplate or chargrill pan (griddle) to medium. Add chicken and cook for 6–8 minutes on one side. Turn and then cook for a further 5 minutes, or until cooked through — cooking time will vary depending on the heat of your barbecue and the thickness of chicken fillets. Remove from heat and leave to cool slightly.

Meanwhile, make the black vinegar dressing. Pour vinegar, kecap manis and soy sauce into a bowl and whisk together. Add the sesame oil and the vegetable oil, whisk well, then stir in the ginger and set aside.

Shred or slice the chicken and toss in a serving bowl with the carrot, baby Asian greens and cucumber. Pour over the dressing and toss gently. Scatter with the bean sprouts, spring onion and basil and serve.

Serves 4

Fattoush

2 pitta bread rounds (17 cm/7 inch
diameter)
6 cos (romaine) lettuce leaves,
shredded
1 large Lebanese (short) cucumber,
cubed
4 tomatoes, cut into 1 cm (½ inch)
cubes
8 spring onions (scallions), chopped
1 large handful, flat-leaf (Italian)
parsley, finely chopped
1 tablespoon finely chopped mint
2 tablespoons finely chopped
coriander (cilantro)

Dressing
2 garlic cloves, crushed
100 ml (4 fl oz) extra virgin olive oil
100 ml (4 fl oz) lemon juice

Preheat the oven to moderate 180°C
(350°F/Gas 4). Split the bread in half
through the centre and then bake on
a baking tray for 8–10 minutes, or
until golden and crisp, turning halfway
through. Break into pieces.

To make the dressing, whisk all the
ingredients together in a bowl until
well combined.

Place the bread and remaining salad
ingredients in a serving bowl and toss
to combine. Drizzle with the dressing
and toss well. Season to taste with
salt and freshly ground black pepper.
Serve immediately.

Serves 6

Beef satay salad

2 teaspoons tamarind pulp
½ teaspoon sesame oil
2 tablespoons soy sauce
2 teaspoons soft brown sugar
2 garlic cloves, crushed
1 tablespoon lime juice
700 g (1 lb 9 oz) rump steak
1 tablespoon peanut oil
6 large cos (romaine) lettuce leaves,
  washed, dried and shredded
1 red capsicum (pepper), julienned
180 g (6 oz/2 cups) bean sprouts
2 tablespoons fried onion flakes

Satay sauce
2 red chillies, chopped
½ teaspoon shrimp paste
1 garlic clove
6 red Asian shallots
2 teaspoons peanut oil
250 ml (9 fl oz/1 cup) coconut milk
1 tablespoon lime juice
120 g (4 oz/¾ cup) unsalted roasted
  peanuts, finely ground in a food
  processor
1 tablespoon kecap manis
1 tablespoon soft brown sugar
1 tablespoon fish sauce
2 makrut lime (kaffir) leaves, shredded

Combine the tamarind pulp and
3 tablespoons of boiling water and
allow to cool. Mash pulp with your
fingertips to dissolve it, then strain,
reserving liquid. Discard pulp. Put
sesame oil, the soy sauce, the sugar,
garlic, lime juice and 2 tablespoons
of tamarind water in a large bowl.
Add steak, turn to coat, and cover
with plastic wrap. Chill for 2 hours.

Meanwhile, to make the satay sauce,
process the chillies, the shrimp paste,
garlic and shallots to a paste in a food
processor. Heat the oil in a frying pan
and cook paste for 3 minutes. Add
coconut milk, lime juice, the ground
peanuts, remaining tamarind water,
kecap manis, sugar, fish sauce and
makrut lime leaves. Cook on medium
heat until thickened, thin with 125 ml
(½ cup) water, and return to the boil
for 2 minutes. Season.

Heat peanut oil in a frying pan over
high heat, and cook the steak for
3 minutes on each side, or until it is
medium–rare. Leave for 3 minutes,
then slice thinly. Toss the steak slices
in a large bowl with lettuce, capsicum
and bean sprouts. Pile onto serving
plates, drizzle with satay sauce and
then sprinkle with fried onion flakes.

Serves 4

Italian tomato salad

6 Roma (plum) tomatoes
2 teaspoons capers, rinsed and
    drained
6 basil leaves, torn
1 tablespoon olive oil
1 tablespoon balsamic vinegar
2 garlic cloves, crushed
1/2 teaspoon honey

Cut the tomatoes lengthways into quarters. Place on a grill tray, skin side down, and cook under a hot griller (broiler) for 4–5 minutes, or until golden. Place in a bowl and cool to room temperature.

Combine the capers, basil leaves, olive oil, balsamic vinegar, crushed garlic and honey in a bowl, season with salt and freshly ground black pepper and pour over the tomatoes. Toss gently.

Serves 6

Thai beef salad

600 g (1 lb 5 oz) beef fillet, trimmed
2 tablespoons fish sauce
1 tablespoons peanut oil
2 vine-ripened tomatoes, each cut
 into 8 wedges
½ butter lettuce, leaves separated

Mint and chilli dressing
1 small dried red chilli, roughly
 chopped
80 ml (3 fl oz/⅓ cup) fish sauce
4 red Asian shallots, finely sliced
2 spring onions (scallions), thinly
 sliced on the diagonal
1 handful mint leaves
1 handful coriander (cilantro) leaves
1 garlic clove, crushed
100 ml (4fl oz) lime juice
2 teaspoons grated palm sugar or
 soft brown sugar

Put the beef in a bowl and pour over the fish sauce. Cover and refrigerate for 3 hours, turning the meat several times to coat.

Put a baking tray in oven and preheat oven to 220°C (425°F/Gas 7). Heat the oil in a frying pan and cook beef fillet over high heat for 1 minute on each side, or until browned, place on the hot baking tray and then roast for 15 minutes for a medium-rare result. Remove from oven, cover loosely with foil and allow to rest for 10 minutes.

Meanwhile, make the mint and chilli dressing. Put a small, non-stick frying pan over medium–high heat. Add the chilli and dry-fry for 1–2 minutes, or until dark but not burnt. Transfer to a mortar or spice mill and grind to a fine powder. Place in bowl with remaining dressing ingredients and stir in sugar until it dissolves.

Thinly slice beef and toss in a bowl with the dressing and the tomatoes. Arrange lettuce on a serving platter and then pile the beef salad on top. Serve warm.

Serves 4

Mexicana salad

250 g (8 oz/1¼ cups) black-eyed
  beans
250 g (8 oz) red kidney beans
500 g (1 lb 2 oz) orange sweet potato
1 large red onion, chopped
1 large green capsicum (pepper),
  chopped
3 ripe tomatoes, chopped
3 tablespoons chopped basil
3 flour tortillas
1 tablespoon oil
2 tablespoons grated parmesan
3 tablespoons sour cream

Dressing
1 clove garlic, crushed
1 tablespoon lime juice
2 tablespoons olive oil

Guacamole
3 avocados
2 tablespoons lemon juice
1 clove garlic, crushed
1 small red onion, chopped
1 small red chilli, chopped
3 tablespoons sour cream
2 tablespoons hot ready-made
  taco sauce

Soak beans in a large bowl of cold
water overnight. Drain and cook in a
large pan of rapidly boiling water for
30 minutes, or until just tender. Skim
off any scum that appears on surface
during cooking. Do not overcook or
they will become mushy. Drain and
set aside to cool.

Chop sweet potato into large pieces
and cook in boiling water until tender.
Drain and combine with capsicum,
onion, tomatoes and beans. Stir in
the basil.

To make dressing, shake ingredients
in a jar until combined. Pour over the
salad and toss to coat.

Preheat the oven to moderate 180°C
(350°F/Gas 4). Using a small knife,
cut cactus shapes or large triangles
out of the tortillas, brush lightly with
the oil and sprinkle with parmesan.
Bake for 5–10 minutes, or until they
are crisp and golden.

To make guacamole, mash avocados
with the lemon juice. Add the garlic,
onion, chilli, sour cream and the taco
sauce and mix well. Pile guacamole in
centre of salad, top with sour cream
and arrange cactus shapes on top.

Serves 10–12

Indian-style lamb couscous salad

250 g (9 oz) lamb backstrap (tender
  eye of the lamb loin)
1 tablespoon mild curry powder
2 tablespoons pepitas (pumpkin
  seeds)
2 tablespoons sesame seeds
2 teaspoons cumin seeds
2 teaspoons coriander seeds
1 tablespoon oil
2 tablespoons lemon juice
1 onion, chopped
1 carrot, chopped
125 g (5 oz) orange sweet potato,
  cubed
1 clove garlic, finely chopped
185 g (6 oz/1 cup) couscous
3 tablespoons raisins

Sprinkle lamb with curry powder and
salt. Coat well. Cover with plastic
wrap. Refrigerate while making salad.

Place pepitas and sesame seeds in a
dry frying pan and cook, stirring, over
medium-high heat until seeds begin
to brown. Add cumin and coriander
seeds and continue stirring until the
pepitas are puffed and begin to pop.
Remove from heat and allow to cool.
Heat oil in a pan, add lamb and cook
over medium heat for 5–8 minutes, or
until browned. Remove from the pan,
drizzle with lemon juice and leave to
cool to room temperature.

In same pan, stir onion, carrot and
sweet potato over high heat until the
onion is translucent. Reduce heat to
medium, add 3 tablespoons water,
cover and cook for 3 minutes, or until
tender. Stir in garlic and the remaining
lemon juice.

Pour 250 ml (8 fl oz/1 cup) boiling
water into a bowl and add couscous.
Mix and leave for 2 minutes, or until
the water has been absorbed. Add
vegetable mixture, raisins and most of
the toasted nuts and seeds, and toss
until combined. Spoon mixture onto a
plate. Slice the lamb and arrange over
salad. Sprinkle with nuts and seeds.

Serves 6

Cherry tomato and chorizo migas

1 chorizo sausage
80 ml (3 fl oz/⅓ cup) olive oil
250 g (9 oz) yellow cherry tomatoes
pinch of paprika
pinch chilli flakes
½ teaspoon cumin seeds
2 garlic cloves, crushed
4 thick slices 2-day-old bread,
  crusts removed, cut into 2 cm
  (¾ inch) cubes

Cut the chorizo into pieces of a similar size to the bread cubes. Heat the olive oil in a large frying pan over high heat. Add the chorizo, tomatoes, paprika, chilli flakes and cumin seeds. Fry, stirring often, for 4 minutes or until browned. Add the garlic and fry for another 20 seconds.

Remove the chorizo mixture from the pan with a slotted spoon and drain on paper towels. Add the bread to the pan and fry for about 4 minutes, until crisp and golden, then remove with a slotted spoon and drain on paper towels. When all the ingredients have cooled, combine in a serving bowl. Serve with toothpicks and napkins.

Serves 4

Kokoda

450 g (1 lb) flounder, skinned
125 ml (4 fl oz/$^1/_2$ cup) lime juice
2 vine-ripened tomatoes
125 ml (4 fl oz/$^1/_2$ cup) coconut milk
1 small red chilli, seeded and finely
   chopped
2 French shallots, thinly sliced
1 clove garlic, crushed
1 small red capsicum (pepper), diced

Cut the fish into small cubes and put in a non-metallic bowl. Add the lime juice and a generous pinch of salt and mix with a non-metallic spoon. Cover and leave to marinate in the refrigerator for at least 4 hours. Stir the fish every hour or so. You can leave the fish to marinate overnight if you prefer.

When fish is ready, prepare the other ingredients. Score a cross in the base of each tomato. Put into boiling water for 20 seconds, then plunge into cold water. Drain and peel skin away from the cross. Dice tomatoes, discarding the cores and seeds.

Mix the tomatoes with the coconut milk, chilli, shallots, garlic and red capsicum. Drain fish and combine with the coconut mixture. Taste to check seasoning, adding more salt if necessary. Eat immediately or chill until required.

Serves 6

Note: Sole, plaice or any delicate white fish can be used as a fish substitution.

Japanese potato salad

500 g (1 lb 2 oz) all-purpose
  potatoes, peeled
50 g (2 oz) sliced ham
1 Lebanese (short) cucumber

Dressing
185 g (7 oz/$^3/_4$ cup) Japanese
  mayonnaise
$^1/_2$ teaspoon Japanese mustard
2 tablespoons Japanese rice vinegar
a few drops sesame oil
2 spring onions (scallions), finely
  chopped
2 large handfuls mitsuba or flat-leaf
  (Italian) parsley, finely chopped, plus
  extra leaves to garnish, optional
ground white pepper, to season

Cut potatoes into 2 cm ($^3/_4$ inch) dice.
Bring a saucepan of salted water to
the boil and add the potato. Cook for
8 minutes, or until tender. Drain, rinse
under cold running water, then drain
again. Lightly crush the potatoes with
a fork but do not mash them — there
should still be some lumps.

Meanwhile, cut ham into thin strips,
about 3 cm (1 $^1/_4$ inch) in length. Cut
 cucumber in half lengthways and
scoop out seeds with a teaspoon,
then slice very thinly.

To make the dressing, combine the
mayonnaise, mustard, the vinegar
and the sesame oil in a bowl. Mix
until smooth, then stir in the spring
onion and mitsuba. Season with salt
and white pepper.

Put the warm potato, ham, cucumber
and the dressing in a bowl and toss
to combine. Set aside for 15 minutes
so the potato can absorb some of
dressing and flavours can develop.
Garnished with extra mitsuba leaves,
if desired.

Serves 6–8

Carpaccio

400 g (14 oz) beef eye fillet
1 tablespoon extra virgin olive oil
rocket (arugula) leaves, torn, to serve
60 g (2 oz) parmesan cheese, shaved,
    to serve
black olives, cut into slivers, to serve

Remove all visible fat and sinew from the beef, then freeze it for 1–2 hours, until firm but not solid. This makes the meat easier to slice thinly.

Cut paper-thin slices of beef with a large, sharp knife. Arrange on a serving platter and allow to return to room temperature.

Just before serving, drizzle with oil, then scatter with rocket, parmesan and olives.

Serves 8

Note: The beef can be cut into slices a few hours in advance, covered and refrigerated. Drizzle with the oil and garnish with the other ingredients just before serving.

Vietnamese prawn salad

1 small Chinese cabbage, finely
  shredded
3 tablespoons sugar
3 tablespoons fish sauce
80 ml (3 fl oz/⅓ cup) lime juice
1 tablespoon white vinegar
1 small red onion, finely sliced
750 g (1 lb 10 oz) cooked tiger
  prawns (shrimp), peeled and
  deveined, tails intact
3 large handfuls coriander (cilantro)
  leaves, chopped
3 large handfuls Vietnamese mint
  leaves, chopped

Place the Chinese cabbage in a large
bowl, cover with plastic wrap and chill
for 30 minutes.

Put the sugar, fish sauce, lime juice,
vinegar and ½ teaspoon salt in a
small jug and mix well.

Toss together the shredded cabbage,
onion, prawns, coriander, mint and
dressing, and garnish with the extra
mint leaves.

Serves 6

Note: Vietnamese mint is available
from Asian grocery stores.

Tandoori chicken salad

4 skinless, boneless chicken breasts
2–3 tablespoons tandoori paste
200 g (7 oz) thick plain yoghurt
1 tablespoon lemon juice
1 large handful coriander (cilantro)
  leaves
60 g (2 oz/½ cup) slivered almonds,
  toasted
snow pea sprouts (mangetout), to
  serve

Cucumber and yoghurt dressing
1 Lebanese (short) cucumber, grated
200 g (7 oz) thick plain yoghurt
1 tablespoon chopped fresh mint
2 teaspoons lemon juice

Cut the chicken breast fillets into thick strips. Combine tandoori paste, the lemon juice and the yoghurt in a large bowl, add the chicken strips and toss to coat well. Refrigerate and leave to marinate overnight.

To make the dressing, put the grated cucumber in a medium bowl. Add the yoghurt, the chopped mint and lemon juice, and stir until well combined. Refrigerate until needed.

Heat a large non-stick frying pan, add the marinated chicken in batches and cook, turning frequently, until cooked through. Cool and place in a bowl. Add coriander leaves and the toasted almonds, and toss until combined. Serve on a bed of snow pea sprouts, with the dressing served separately.

Serves 4

Note: The quality of tandoori paste used will determine the flavour and look of the chicken. There are many home-made varieties available from supermarkets and delicatessens.

Minced pork and noodle salad

1 tablespoon peanut oil
500 g (1 lb 2 oz) minced (ground) pork
2 garlic cloves, finely chopped
1 stem lemongrass, finely chopped
2–3 red Asian shallots, thinly sliced
3 teaspoons finely grated ginger
1 small red chilli, finely chopped
5 makrut lime (kaffir) leaves, very finely shredded
170 g (6 oz) glass (mung bean) noodles
60 g (2 oz) baby English spinach leaves
4 large handfuls coriander (cilantro), roughly chopped
170 g (6 oz/1 cup) peeled, finely chopped fresh pineapple
1 handful mint leaves

Dressing
1½ tablespoons shaved palm sugar or soft brown sugar
2 tablespoons fish sauce
80 ml (3 fl oz/⅓ cup) lime juice
2 teaspoons sesame oil
2 teaspoons peanut oil

Heat a wok until very hot, add the peanut oil and swirl to coat the wok. Add pork and stir-fry in batches over high heat for 5 minutes, or until lightly golden. Add garlic, lemongrass, chilli, shallots, the grated ginger and lime leaves, and then stir-fry for a further 1–2 minutes, or until fragrant.

Place noodles in a bowl and cover with boiling water for 30 seconds, or until softened. Rinse under cold water and drain well. Toss in a bowl with the spinach, coriander, pineapple, mint and pork mixture.

To make the dressing, mix together the palm sugar, fish sauce and lime juice. Add the sesame oil and extra peanut oil, and whisk to combine. Toss through the salad and season with freshly ground black pepper.

Serves 4

Tunisian carrot salad

500 g (1 lb 2 oz) carrots
3 tablespoons finely chopped flat-leaf
  (Italian) parsley
1 teaspoon ground cumin
80 ml (3 fl oz/⅓ cup) olive oil
3 tablespoons red wine vinegar
2 garlic cloves, crushed
¼–½ teaspoon ready-made harissa
  (see Notes)
12 black olives
2 hard-boiled eggs, quartered

Thinly slice the carrots. Bring 500 ml (17 fl oz/2 cups) water to the boil in a saucepan. Add the carrot and cook until tender. Drain and then transfer to a bowl. Add parsley, cumin, garlic, vinegar and olive oil. Season with the harissa and salt and pepper. Stir well.

Put the carrots in a serving dish and garnish with the olives and egg.

Serves 6

Notes: If the carrots are not sweet, add a little honey to the dressing. Harissa is a spicy paste blend available from delicatessens.

Something
Special

Scallop ceviche

16 scallops, on the half-shell
1 teaspoon finely grated lime zest,
   plus extra strips of lime zest,
   to serve
2 garlic cloves, chopped
2 small red chillies, seeded and finely
   chopped
125 ml (4 fl oz/½ cup) lime juice
1–2 tablespoons chopped parsley
1 tablespoons olive oil

Remove the scallops from their shells and reserve the shells. You may need to use a small, sharp knife to slice the scallops free — be careful not to leave any scallop meat behind. Slice or pull off any vein, membrane or hard white muscle, leaving any roe attached. Rinse the scallops and pat them dry with paper towels.

In a large non-metallic bowl, mix together the remaining ingredients and then season with salt and freshly ground black pepper. Add scallops and gently stir to coat. Cover with plastic wrap and then refrigerate for 2 hours, or up to 1 day — during this time acid in the lime juice will 'cook' the scallops, firming the flesh and turning it opaque.

To serve, slide each scallop back onto a half-shell and spoon the dressing over. Scatter with lime zest strips and enjoy cold as a starter salad.

Serves 4

Roasted vegetables with pan-fried garlic breadcrumbs

3 zucchini (courgettes), sliced
225 g (8 oz) button mushrooms,
  larger ones halved
1 red onion, cut into 8 wedges
1 red capsicum (pepper), diced
3 tablespoons olive oil
1 garlic clove, crushed
40 g (1½ oz/½ cup) breadcrumbs,
  made from day-old bread

Dressing
1 tablespoon olive oil
2 tablespoons ready-made pesto
1 tablespoon lemon juice

Preheat oven to 200°C (400°F/Gas 6). Put all vegetables in a large baking dish. Drizzle over 2 tablespoons of the oil, add salt and pepper and shake pan to coat all the vegetables in the oil. Roast for 30 minutes, or until all the vegetables are tender.

Combine the dressing ingredients in a large serving bowl. Add the roasted vegetables, toss gently and leave for 10 minutes for the flavours to absorb.

Heat the remaining oil in a frying pan and fry the garlic over medium heat for about 30 seconds. Increase the heat, add the breadcrumbs and fry for 2–3 minutes, or until golden, shaking the pan and stirring the crumbs. Toss the toasted breadcrumbs through the salad and serve.

Serves 4

Crab, cucumber and wakame salad

2 Lebanese (short) cucumbers
2 tablespoons dried wakame
  seaweed pieces
150 g (6 oz/1 cup) fresh crabmeat,
  cooked, picked over (or good
  quality tinned crabmeat)

Dressing
2 tablespoons Japanese rice vinegar
½ teaspoon dashi granules
1 tablespoon shoyu (Japanese soy
  sauce)
2 teaspoons mirin
20 g (¾ oz) ginger

Dissolve 2 teaspoons salt in 500 ml (17 fl oz/2 cups) cold water. Cut the cucumbers in half lengthways, scoop out the seeds, then slice the flesh very thinly. Put cucumber flesh in cold water and soak for 10 minutes. Drain well and squeeze out extra moisture. Keep in refrigerator until needed.

Soak wakame in a bowl of cold water for 5 minutes, or until rehydrated and glossy but not mushy. Drain well, then refrigerate until needed.

To make the dashi, mix the granules with 1½ tablespoons of hot water. To make dressing, combine rice vinegar, dashi, shoyu and the mirin in a small saucepan and bring to the boil over high heat. Remove from heat and cool to room temperature. Finely grate the ginger, then squeeze grated ginger with fingertips to release the juice (you will need 1½ teaspoons of the ginger juice). Add ginger juice to the dressing and stir well. Allow to cool completely and then refrigerate for 15 minutes, or until cold.

Neatly arrange cucumber, wakame and crabmeat in four small serving dishes, then carefully pour dressing over the top.

Serves 4

Smoked mackerel salad with horseradish, watercress and green beans

400 g (14 oz) medium-sized potatoes, cut into thick slices
150 g (6 oz) green beans, trimmed
100 g (4 oz) watercress or mixed salad leaves
1 fennel bulb (250 g/9 oz), halved and thinly sliced
1 tablespoon coarsely chopped tarragon, optional
salt and pepper, to taste
1 tablespoon lemon juice or white wine vinegar
2 tablespoons extra virgin olive oil
200 g (7 oz) peeled cooked fresh beetroot, thickly sliced then cut into strips
4 heaped teaspoons low-fat bio (plain) yoghurt
4 heaped teaspoons freshly grated horseradish or hot horseradish sauce
4 fillets (350 g/12 oz) smoked mackerel, skinned, boned and cut into large strips

Cook the potatoes in boiling salted water for about 10 minutes, until tender. Meanwhile, steam the green beans for 2 minutes, until bright green and just tender. Drain the beans and set aside to dry.

Place the watercress or salad leaves in a large salad bowl, then add the sliced fennel, potatoes, green beans, and tarragon if using. Season with salt and pepper, drizzle over lemon juice or vinegar and olive oil, and mix well.

Just before serving, add the beetroot and mix briefly, to prevent beetroot discolouring the other vegetables.

Mix the yoghurt with the horseradish and set aside. Place the salad on the individual plates and scatter over the mackerel pieces. Place a dollop of the horseradish dressing on top and then serve immediately.

Serves 4

Chargrilled polenta with shaved fennel salad

500 ml (17 fl oz/2 cups) milk
175 g (6 oz) polenta (cornmeal) (don't
  use instant polenta)
35 g (1 oz/⅓ cup) grated parmesan
  cheese, plus
100 g (4 oz/1 cup) shaved parmesan
  cheese
1 tablespoons butter
2 baby fennel bulbs, trimmed (reserve
  the fronds)
40 g (2 oz/1⅓ cups) watercress
  leaves
3 teaspoons lemon juice
1½ tablespoons olive oil

Bring the milk and 500 ml (17 fl oz/ 2 cups) water to the boil in a heavy-based saucepan. Add the polenta in a thin, steady stream and whisk thoroughly. Reduce the heat as low as possible and then simmer for 30–40 minutes, stirring occasionally. Remove from heat, stir in the grated parmesan and butter and season well. Pour into an oiled square dish and leave for 30 minutes to set.

When cold, cut into four squares, then cut each square diagonally to give eight triangles. Brush with a little oil and cook on a hot chargrill pan (griddle) or barbecue hotplate until crisp brown grill marks appear.

Slice the fennel very thinly and chop the fronds. Toss in a bowl with the watercress, lemon juice, oil and half the shaved parmesan. Season well. Stack two polenta triangles on four serving plates, pile the salad on top, scatter with the remaining shaved parmesan and serve.

Serves 4

Baby beetroot and tatsoi salad with honey mustard dressing

1.6 kg (3 lb 8 oz) baby beetroot
250 g (9 oz/1²/₃ cups) broad (fava)
   beans (from 500 g/1 lb 2 oz/3 cups
   fresh broad beans in the pod)
200 g (7 oz/1 bunch) tatsoi

Dressing
80 ml (2½ fl oz/⅓ cup) olive oil
1 tablespoon lemon juice
1 tablespoon wholegrain mustard
1 tablespoon honey

Wearing rubber gloves, trim beetroot, discarding the stalks but reserving the unblemished leaves. Bring a medium saucepan of water to the boil. Add the beetroot and simmer, covered, for 8–10 minutes, or until tender, then drain. Ease off the skins, pat dry with paper towels and rinse. Put beetroot in a large shallow bowl.

Bring a small saucepan of water to the boil, add a large pinch of salt and the broad beans, and simmer for 2–3 minutes, then drain. When cool enough to handle, slip the beans out of their skins and add to the beetroot. Add the reserved beetroot leaves and the small inner leaves of the tatsoi.

To make the dressing, place all the dressing ingredients in a small bowl and whisk to combine. Season with salt and freshly ground black pepper. Pour over the beetroot mixture and toss gently. Serve warm.

Serves 4

Roasted fennel, beetroot and smoked trout salad

12 baby beetroot
2–3 tablespoons olive oil
2 large fennel bulbs
100 g (3½ oz) smoked trout fillet,
  broken into chunks
crusty bread, to serve

Horseradish dressing
175 g (6 oz/²/₃ cup) sour cream
1 tablespoons creamed horseradish
1 tablespoons lemon juice
2 tablespoons snipped chives

Preheat oven to 200°C (400°F/Gas 6). Wearing gloves, peel beetroot, then cut the bulbs into chunks. Place in a large roasting tin and then drizzle with 2 tablespoons of the oil. Season with salt and black pepper and then toss to coat, cover with foil and roast for 40–45 minutes, or until tender.

Meanwhile, cut off and discard stalks and fronds from the fennel. Cut bulbs into quarters and blanch in boiling salted water for 5 minutes, or until tender. Drain well and cut into smaller wedges. Add to beetroot for the final 30 minutes of cooking, adding a little extra oil if needed.

Put beetroot and fennel in a serving dish with the smoked trout. Combine the horseradish dressing ingredients in a small bowl and dollop over the salad. Serve warm with crusty bread.

Serves 4

Goat's cheese, avocado and smoked salmon salad

2 tablespoons extra virgin olive oil
1 tablespoons balsamic vinegar
40 g (2 oz) baby rocket (arugula)
1 avocado
100 g (4 oz) smoked salmon pieces,
  sliced (see Note)
8 rounds of marinated goat's cheese,
  drained
2 tablespoons roasted hazelnuts,
  coarsely chopped

In a large bowl, whisk together the oil and vinegar and season to taste.

Cut the avocado lengthways into quarters, then discard the skin. Place an avocado quarter on each serving plate and arrange a pile of rocket and smoked salmon over top.

Stack two goat's cheese rounds on each plate and scatter hazelnuts over the top. Drizzle dressing over, season with a good grind of black pepper and serve at once.

Serves 4

Note: A whole smoked trout can be used instead of the salmon. Peel away the skin, remove the bones, then flake the flesh into bite-sized pieces.

Scallop, ginger and spinach salad

300 g (11 oz) scallops, without roe
oil, for brushing
100 g (4 oz) baby English spinach
    leaves
1 small red capsicum (pepper), very
    finely julienned
50 g (1³/₄ oz/¹/₂ cup) bean sprouts,
    tails trimmed

Sake dressing
25 ml (1 fl oz) sake
1 tablespoon lime juice
2 teaspoons shaved palm sugar, or
    soft brown sugar
1 teaspoon fish sauce

Slice or pull off any vein, membrane or
hard white muscle from the scallops.
Rinse scallops and pat dry with paper
towels. Put all dressing ingredients in
a small bowl and mix until the sugar
has dissolved.

Heat a chargrill pan (griddle) or
barbecue hotplate to high and lightly
brush with oil. Cook the scallops in
batches for 1 minute on each side,
or until just cooked.

Divide spinach, capsicum and bean
sprouts between four plates. Arrange
scallops on top, pour over dressing
and serve at once.

Serves 4

Marinated grilled tofu salad with ginger miso dressing

80 ml (3 fl oz/⅓ cup) tamari, shoyu or
  light soy sauce
2 teaspoons oil
2 garlic cloves, crushed
1 teaspoon grated fresh ginger
1 teaspoon chilli paste
500 g (1 lb 2 oz) firm tofu, cut into
  2 cm (¾ inch) cubes
400 g (14 oz) mixed salad leaves
1 Lebanese (short) cucumber, finely
  sliced
250 g (9 oz) cherry tomatoes, halved
2 teaspoons oil, extra

Dressing
2 teaspoons white miso paste
2 tablespoons mirin
1 teaspoon sesame oil
1 teaspoon grated fresh ginger
1 teaspoon finely chopped chives
1 tablespoon toasted sesame seeds

Mix together the tamari, oil, garlic,
ginger, chilli paste and ½ teaspoon
salt in a bowl. Add the tofu and mix
until well coated. Marinate for at least
10 minutes, or preferably overnight.
Drain and reserve the marinade.

To make the dressing, combine the
miso with 125 ml (½ cup) hot water
and leave until the miso dissolves.
Add the mirin, sesame oil, ginger,
chives and sesame seeds and stir
thoroughly until it begins to thicken.

Combine the mixed salad leaves,
cucumber and tomato in a serving
bowl and leave until ready to serve.

Heat the extra oil in a chargrill pan or
barbecue hotplate. Add the tofu and
cook over medium heat for 4 minutes,
or until golden brown. Pour on the
reserved marinade and then cook
for 1 minute over high heat. Remove
from chargrill and allow to cool for
5 minutes. Add tofu to salad, drizzle
with the dressing and toss well.

Serves 4

Note: Miso is Japanese bean paste
and plays an important part in their
cuisine. It is commonly used in soups,
dressings, on grilled (broiled) foods
and as a flavouring for pickles.

Wild rice salad with Chinese roast duck

200 g (7 oz/1 cup) wild rice
200 g (7 oz/1 cup) basmati or
  jasmine rice
16 thin asparagus spears, woody
  ends trimmed, sliced
8 spring onions (scallions), thinly
  sliced
100 g (3$\frac{1}{2}$ oz) pecans, roughly
  chopped
100 g (3$\frac{1}{2}$ oz) dried cranberries
zest and juice of 1 orange
1 whole Chinese roast duck

Dressing
125 ml (4 fl oz/$\frac{1}{2}$ cup) soy sauce
2 tablespoons sugar
1$\frac{1}{2}$ tablespoons balsamic vinegar
1$\frac{1}{2}$ tablespoons peanut oil
2 teaspoons sesame oil
2 teaspoons grated fresh ginger
2 small red chillies, finely chopped

Put the wild rice in a saucepan of cold salted water, bring to the boil and cook for 30 minutes. Add the basmati or jasmine rice and continue to cook for a further 10 minutes, or until both rices are just cooked. Drain and refresh under cold water, then drain again and transfer to a large bowl.

Blanch the asparagus in a saucepan of boiling water, then drain and refresh under cold water. Add to the bowl with the rice. Add the spring onion, pecans, dried cranberries and orange zest to the rice and mix together well.

Combine all the dressing ingredients and the orange juice in a screw-top jar and shake well.

Preheat the oven to 200°C(400°F/ Gas 6). Remove the skin from the duck and break it into rough pieces. Shred the duck meat and add it to the salad. Put the skin on a baking tray and bake for 5 minutes, or until crispy. Drain on paper towel, then slice.

If necessary, shake the dressing again before pouring it over the salad. Toss to combine. Serve the salad in individual bowls, topped with pieces of crispy duck skin.

Serves 4–6

Smoked trout Caesar salad

350 g (12 oz) skinless smoked trout
  fillets
300 g (10½ oz) green beans, halved
6 tinned artichokes, drained, rinsed
  and quartered
2 eggs
1 small garlic clove, chopped
2 teaspoons Dijon mustard
2 tablespoons white wine vinegar
80 ml (3 fl oz/⅓ cup) olive oil
6 slices (200 g/7 oz) day-old Italian-
  style bread (ciabatta), cut into 2 cm
  (¾ inch) cubes
2 tablespoons capers, drained
1 baby cos (romaine) lettuce, leaves
  separated
40 g (1 oz/½ cup) freshly shaved
  parmesan cheese

Flake the trout into 4 cm (1½ inch) shards and place in a bowl. Cook the beans in boiling water for 3 minutes, or until tender and still bright green. Refresh under cold water. Add to the bowl, with the artichoke.

Poach the eggs in simmering water for 40 seconds, or until just cooked. Place in a food processor with garlic, mustard and vinegar, and process until smooth. With the motor running, add 2 tablespoons oil in a thin stream, processing until thick and creamy. Season to taste.

Heat the remaining oil in a frying pan, add the bread and capers, and cook over high heat for 3–5 minutes, or until golden. Line four bowls with the cos leaves. Divide the trout mixture among the bowls, drizzle with the dressing and top with the croutons, capers and parmesan.

Serves 4

Cheese, walnut and spiced pear salad

2 large pears
100 ml (3½ fl oz) balsamic vinegar
100 ml (3½ fl oz) red wine
pinch of ground cinnamon
1 star anise
pinch of Chinese five spice
2 heaped teaspoons brown or
 unrefined brown sugar
100 g (3½ oz) watercress and/or
 spinach
3 tablespoons walnut, pumpkin seed
 or extra virgin olive oil
1 tablespoon balsamic vinegar,
 optional
200 g (7 oz) soft blue cheese, such
 as dolcelatte or roquefort, cut into
 small cubes
100 g (3½ oz) fresh walnuts, lightly
 toasted
4 thin slices of toasted walnut or
 wholemeal bread, to serve

Peel and cut the pears into quarters, remove the cores and cut again into eighths. Place in a small saucepan and add the balsamic vinegar, wine, cinnamon, star anise or Chinese five spice, and sugar. Cover with a circle of greaseproof paper, bring to the boil and simmer gently for15 minutes until the pears are soft. Set aside to cool, then place in a bowl or glass jar until needed. Discard liquid before serving.

Place watercress and/or spinach in a bowl with the oil, balsamic vinegar if using, and salt and pepper. Mix to coat the leaves, then add the cheese, walnuts and pear slices to the bowl, or serve on individual plates. Serve with the toast.

Serves 4

Note: A 200 g (7 oz) jar of spiced or pickled pears, drained, can be substituted for cooked fresh pears if preferred.

Chargrilled baby octopus salad

1 kg (2 lb 4 oz) baby octopus
1 teaspoon sesame oil
2 tablespoons lime juice
2 tablespoons fish sauce
2 tablespoons sweet chilli sauce
200 g (7 oz) mixed salad leaves
1 red capsicum (pepper), very thinly sliced
2 small Lebanese (short) cucumbers, seeded and cut into ribbons
4 red Asian shallots, chopped
100 g (3½ oz) toasted unsalted peanuts, chopped

To clean the octopus, remove the head from the tentacles by cutting just underneath the eyes. To clean the head, carefully slit the head open and remove the gut. Cut it in half. Push out the beak from the centre of the tentacles, then cut the tentacles into sets of four or two, depending on their size. Pull the skin away from the head and tentacles if it comes away easily. The eyes will come off as you pull off the skin.

To make the marinade, combine the sesame oil, lime juice, fish sauce and chilli sauce in a shallow, non-metallic bowl. Add octopus, and stir to coat. Cover and chill for 2 hours. Heat a chargrill pan or barbecue hotplate to hot. Drain the octopus, reserving the marinade, then cook in batches for 3–5 minutes, turning occasionally.

Pour the reserved marinade into a small saucepan, bring to the boil and cook for 2 minutes, or until it has thickened slightly.

Divide the salad leaves among four plates, scatter with capsicum and cucumber, then top with octopus. Drizzle with marinade and top with the Asian shallots and peanuts.

Serves 3–4

Crab salad with green mango and coconut

Dressing
2 garlic cloves, peeled
1 small red chilli
1½ tablespoons dried shrimp
1½ tablespoons fish sauce
2 tablespoons lime juice
2 teaspoon palm sugar or soft brown
   sugar

4 tablespoons shredded coconut
   (see Note)
200 g (7 oz/2 cups) shredded green
   mango (see Note)
1 small handful mint leaves (torn if
   very big)
1 small handful coriander (cilantro)
   leaves
2 lime (kaffir) leaves, shredded
1½ teaspoon thinly shredded pickled
   ginger
350 g (12 oz) fresh crabmeat
4 small squares banana leaves
   (optional)
50 g (2 oz/⅓ cup) chopped toasted
   unsalted peanuts
4 lime wedges

Preheat oven to 180°C (350°F/Gas 4). To make dressing, pound the garlic, chilli, dried shrimp and ½ teaspoon salt to a paste in a mortar. Whisk in the fish sauce, lime juice and sugar with a fork.

Spread the shredded coconut on a baking tray and bake for 1–2 minutes, shaking tray occasionally to ensure even toasting. Watch coconut closely, as it will burn easily.

Put the shredded mango in a large bowl and add the mint, coriander, lime leaves, ginger, coconut and crabmeat meat. Pour dressing over the top and toss together gently.

If using banana leaves, place a square in each serving bowl (leaves are for presentation only and are not edible). Mound some crab salad on the top, sprinkle with the peanuts and serve immediately with lime wedges.

Serves 4

Note: Freshly shredded coconut is delicious, so if you have time, remove the skin from a coconut and shred the flesh using a vegetable peeler. For this recipe you will need 3 green mangoes to get the right quantity of shredded mango flesh.

Sprout and pear salad with sesame dressing

250 g (9 oz) snow pea (mangetout)
  sprouts
250 g (9 oz) bean sprouts
30 g (1 oz) chives
100 g (3½ oz) snow peas (mangetout)
1 celery stalk
2 firm pears (not green)
coriander (cilantro) sprigs
sesame seeds, to garnish

Sesame dressing
2 tablespoons soy sauce
1 teaspoon sesame oil
1 tablespoon soft brown sugar
2 tablespoons peanut oil
1 tablespoon rice vinegar

Wash and drain snow pea sprouts. Remove the brown tips from bean sprouts. Snip the chives into 4 cm (1½ inch) lengths and cut snow peas and celery into thin matchstick strips.

Peel and core pears, then slice into thin strips, slightly wider than the celery and snow peas. Place in a bowl and cover with water to stop discoloration.

To make sesame dressing, combine the ingredients and mix thoroughly.

Drain the pears. Combine all the salad ingredients and the coriander sprigs in a large serving bowl. Pour dressing over and toss lightly.

Sprinkle with sesame seeds and then serve immediately.

Serves 6

Scallop salad with saffron dressing

Saffron dressing
pinch of saffron threads
60 g (3 oz/⅓ cup) ready-made
  mayonnaise
1½ tablespoons cream
1 teaspoon lemon juice

20 scallops, with roe
25 g (1 oz) butter
1 tablespoons olive oil
100 g (4 oz) mixed salad leaves
1 small handful chervil leaves

To make the saffron dressing, put the saffron in a bowl and soak in 2 teaspoons of hot water for about 10 minutes. Add mayonnaise, mixing well, until the mixture becomes a rich yellow in colour. Stir in cream, then lemon juice. Refrigerate until needed.

Slice or pull off any vein, membrane or hard white muscle from the scallops, leaving the roe attached. Rinse the scallops and pat them dry with paper towels. Heat the butter and oil in a large frying pan over high heat and sear the scallops in small batches for 1 minute on each side.

Divide the salad leaves and chervil between four serving plates, then top each with five scallops. Drizzle the dressing over the top and serve.

Serves 4

Poached egg salad with bacon, capsicum and croutons

2 red capsicums (peppers)
150 g (5½ oz) mixed salad leaves,
   such as cos and watercress
4 spring onions, trimmed and finely
   sliced
1 large ripe avocado, quartered and
   sliced
4 medium-sized slices wholemeal
   bread
1 clove garlic, peeled and cut
   in half
1 tablespoon sunflower oil
8 rashers smoked bacon
dash of vinegar
4 eggs

Dressing
2 teaspoons Dijon mustard
1 tablespoon white wine vinegar or
   lemon juice
4 tablespoons extra-extra virgin
   olive oil

Grill capsicums (peppers) until black, and place in a sealed plastic bag to cool. Remove skin and seeds, then cut into strips. Place salad leaves in a large salad bowl and add the onions, avocado and peppers. Toast bread and rub both sides with the garlic. Cut into 2 cm (½ inch) cubes and add to the salad. Heat oil in a frying pan and cook the bacon rashers until golden brown. Drain on kitchen towels.

To make dressing, place the mustard and vinegar or lemon juice in a small jug or bowl and whisk to combine. Add the oil and whisk again.

Bring a saucepan of salted water to a gentle boil. Pour in a dash of vinegar. Gently break an egg into a small bowl or cup and then pour carefully into the water. Repeat quickly with other eggs and simmer gently for 3 minutes for a softly poached egg. (Alternatively, cook in an egg poacher.) Remove the eggs with a slotted spoon and drain briefly on kitchen towel.

Pour dressing over salad, season with salt and black pepper, and toss to coat. Place the bacon and eggs on top and serve.

Serves 4

Pepper-crusted salmon salad

1 tablespoon black pepper, coarsely ground
4 salmon fillets (about 180 g/6 oz each), skin removed
80 g (3 oz/⅓ cup) ready-made mayonnaise
1½ tablespoons lemon juice
2 teaspoons creamed horseradish
1 small garlic clove, crushed
2 tablespoons chopped parsley
100 g (4 oz/3 heaped cups) watercress
3 tablespoons olive oil
25 g (1 oz) butter
8 butter lettuce leaves, torn

Mix the pepper in a bowl with ¼ teaspoon salt. Use the mixture to coat both sides of each salmon fillet, pressing the pepper down firmly with your fingers. Cover and refrigerate for 30 minutes.

Put mayonnaise in a food processor with the lemon juice, the horseradish, garlic, parsley, half the watercress, 1 tablespoon of oil and 1 tablespoon of warm water. Blend for 1 minute.

Heat butter and 1 tablespoon of the oil in a large frying pan until bubbling. Add the salmon fillets and cook over medium heat for about 2–3 minutes on each side for medium-rare, or until cooked to your liking. Remove from the pan and allow to cool slightly.

Arrange lettuce in the middle of four serving plates and drizzle lightly with the remaining oil. Break each salmon fillet into four pieces and arrange over the lettuce. Scatter watercress over the top, pour the dressing over and serve at once.

Serves 4

Roast duck salad with chilli dressing

Chilli dressing
½ teaspoon chilli flakes
2½ tablespoons fish sauce
1 tablespoons lime juice
2 teaspoons grated palm sugar or soft brown sugar

1 Chinese roasted duck
1 small red onion, thinly sliced
1 tablespoon julienned fresh ginger
4 tablespoons roughly chopped mint
4 tablespoons roughly chopped mint
80 g (3 oz/½ cup) roasted unsalted cashew nuts
8 butter lettuce leaves

To make the chilli dressing, put the chilli flakes in a frying pan and dry-fry over medium heat for 30 seconds, then grind to a powder in a mortar or spice grinder. Put the powder in a small bowl with the fish sauce, lime juice and sugar; mix well to dissolve the sugar and set aside.

Remove the flesh from the duck, cut it into bite-sized pieces and put it in a bowl. Add onion, ginger, coriander, mint and cashews. Pour in dressing and toss together gently.

Arrange lettuce on a serving platter, or use the leaves to line individual serving bowls. Top with duck salad and serve.

Serves 4

Spinach salad with bacon and quail eggs

12 quail eggs
2½ tablespoons oil
4 rashers of back bacon or middle
   rashers, cut into thin strips
2 tablespoons apple cider vinegar
2 garlic cloves, crushed
1 teaspoon Dijon mustard
1 teaspoon maple syrup
½ teaspoon Worcestershire sauce
250 g (9 oz) baby English spinach
   leaves
200 g (7 oz) cherry tomatoes, halved
50 g (2 oz/⅓ cup) toasted pine nuts

Bring a small saucepan of water to the boil. Carefully add the quail eggs and simmer for 1½ minutes. Drain, then refresh under cold running water until cool. Carefully peel the eggs and cut them in half.

Heat a little of the oil in a non-stick frying pan. Add the bacon and gently cook for 5 minutes, or until crisp. Remove with tongs, leaving the oil behind, and drain on crumpled paper towels. Add vinegar, garlic, mustard, maple syrup and the Worcestershire sauce to the pan and gently swirl for 2 minutes, or until bubbling. Add the remaining oil and heat for 1 minute.

Layer spinach, bacon, tomatoes and pine nuts in a salad bowl. Add the quail eggs, pour the warm dressing over, season to taste and serve.

Serves 4

Green olive, walnut and pomegranate salad

1 large red onion
100 g (4 oz/1 cup) walnut halves
350 g (12 oz/2 cups) green olives, pitted and halved
175 g (6 oz/1 cup) pomegranate seeds
20 g (3/4 oz) flat-leaf (Italian) parsley leaves

Dressing
125 ml (4 fl oz/1/2 cup) olive oil
1 1/2 tablespoons pomegranate syrup
1/2 teaspoon chilli flakes

Chop onion. Soak the walnut halves in boiling water for 3–4 minutes, or until the skins peel off readily. Drain, peel and pat dry. Lightly toast the walnuts under a medium grill (broiler) and, when cool, roughly chop.

To make the dressing, combine all the ingredients and mix thoroughly.

Put the olives, pomegranate seeds, onion, walnuts and parsley in a bowl and toss. Just before serving, pour over the dressing, season to taste, and combine well.

Serves 4

Rock lobster and mango salad

1 x 800 g (1 lb 12 oz) live rock lobster
100 g (3½ oz) sugar snap peas, trimmed
1 large mango, cut into small chunks
2 spring onions (scallions), trimmed and sliced into small pieces on the diagonal
½ orange capsicum (pepper), thinly sliced
½ Lebanese cucumber, peeled, seeded and sliced into long thin batons

Dressing
zest and juice of 2 limes
1 tablespoon Thai fish sauce
1 small red chilli, seeded and finely chopped
2 tablespoons olive oil
1 teaspoon sesame oil
1 teaspoon dark soy sauce
½ teaspoon sugar

Immobilize rock lobster by placing it in the freezer for 1 hour. Bring a large saucepan of salted water to the boil. Drop lobster into the water and bring back to the boil. Cook for 25 minutes, by which time the lobster will have turned red. Lift out of pan and leave to cool. Once cold, remove cooked meat from the shell. First, remove the head by twisting or cutting it off. Cut down the centre of the underside of the tail with a pair of kitchen scissors. Peel open tail and carefully pull out flesh in one piece. Cut into chunks and place in a large bowl.

Bring a small saucepan of water to the boil, add sugar snap peas and blanch for 2 minutes. Refresh under cold running water, pat dry and add to the lobster flesh with the mango, spring onions, capsicum and cucumber.

Mix the dressing ingredients together in a jug and pour over the lobster and mango. Toss everything together and serve.

Serves 4

Asian prawn and noodle salad

Dressing
2 tablespoons ginger, grated
2 tablespoons soy sauce
2 tablespoons sesame oil
80 ml (3 fl oz/⅓ cup) red wine vinegar
1 tablespoon sweet chilli sauce
2 cloves garlic, crushed
80 ml (3 fl oz/⅓ cup) kecap manis

250 g (9 oz) dried instant egg noodles
500 g (1 lb 2 oz) cooked large prawns
   (shrimp), peeled and deveined, tails
   intact
5 spring onions (scallions), sliced on
   the diagonal
2 tablespoons chopped coriander
   (cilantro)
1 red capsicum (pepper), diced
100 g (3½ oz) snow peas
   (mangetout), cut into halves
lime wedges to serve

For the dressing, whisk together the ginger, soy sauce, sesame oil, vinegar, chilli sauce, garlic and kecap manis in a large bowl.

Cook the egg noodles in a large saucepan of boiling water for about 2 minutes, or until tender, then drain well. Cool in a large serving bowl.

Add the dressing, prawns, spring onions, coriander, capsicum and snow peas to the noodles and toss gently. Serve with the lime wedges.

Serves 4

Smoked salmon and rocket salad

Dressing
2 tablespoons extra virgin olive oil
1 tablespoon balsamic vinegar

150 g (6 oz) rocket (arugula)
1 avocado, cut into 12 wedges
250 g (9 oz) smoked salmon
325 g (12 oz) marinated goat's
  cheese, drained and crumbled
2 tablespoons roasted hazelnuts,
  roughly chopped

To make dressing, thoroughly whisk together the olive oil and vinegar in a bowl. Season to taste. Trim the long stems from the rocket. Rinse leaves, pat dry and toss with the dressing.

Place 3 wedges of avocado on each serving plate, then divide the salmon and rocket among the plates. Scatter the goat's cheese and hazelnuts over the top. Season with freshly ground black pepper.

Serves 4

Index

INDEX

INDEX

Published in 2010 by Murdoch Books Pty Limited

Murdoch Books Australia
Pier 8/9, 23 Hickson Road
Millers Point NSW 2000
Phone: +61 (0)2 8220 2000
Fax: +61 (0)2 8220 2558
www.murdochbooks.com.au

Murdoch Books UK Limited
Erico House, 6th Floor
93–99 Upper Richmond Road
Putney, London SW15 2TG
Phone: +44 (0)20 8785 5995
Fax: +44 (0)20 8785 5985
www.murdochbooks.co.uk

Chief Executive: Juliet Rogers

Publisher: Lynn Lewis
Senior Designer: Heather Menzies
Photography (cover): Stuart Scott
Stylist (cover): Louise Bickle
Editorial Coordinator: Liz Malcolm
Production: Kita George

National Library of Australia Cataloguing-in-Publication Data
Title: Salads.
ISBN: 978-1-74196-951-1 (pbk.)
Series: New chubbie.
Notes: Includes index.
Subjects: Salads.
Dewey Number: 641.83

Cover credits: Red fish dish, Dinosaur Designs. White pasta plate, White Home.
Green fabric and floral print fabric, No Chintz. Red rectangular dish and khaki dish, Mud Australia

Printed by 1010 Printing International.
PRINTED IN CHINA

IMPORTANT: Those who might be at risk from the effects of salmonella poisoning (the elderly, pregnant
women, young children and those suffering from immune deficiency diseases) should consult their doctor
with any concerns about eating raw eggs.

OVEN GUIDE: You may find cooking times vary depending on the oven you are using. For fan-forced
ovens, as a general rule, set the oven temperature to 20°C (35°F) lower than indicated in the recipe.